Cocos2d-x by Example Beginner's Guide

Make fun games for any platform using C++, combined with one of the most popular open source frameworks in the world

Roger Engelbert

BIRMINGHAM - MUMBAI

Cocos2d-x by Example Beginner's Guide

First published: April 2013

Production Reference: 1190413

Published by Packt Publishing Ltd.
Livery Place
35 Livery Street
Birmingham B3 2PB, UK.

ISBN 978-1-78216-734-1

www.packtpub.com

Cover Image by Roger Engelbert (rengelbert@gmail.com)

Credits

Author

Roger Engelbert

Reviewers

Fabio Cunha

Stelios Pallis

Marcio Valenzuela P

Acquisition Editor

Martin Bell

Lead Technical Editor

Joel Noronha

Technical Editors

Veronica Fernandes

Ishita Malhi

Saijul Shah

Project Coordinator

Abhishek Kori

Proofreader

Dirk Manuel

Indexers

Rekha Nair

Monica Ajmera Mehta

Graphics

Valentina D'silva

Production Coordinator

Prachali Bhiwandkar

Cover Work

Prachali Bhiwandkar

About the Author

Roger Engelbert is a game developer with over ten years of experience in developing online games. He grew up surrounded by video games and thinks of classic, 8-bit arcade titles as a form of art. He is the author behind the blog *Done With Computers*, which is chock-full of tutorials on game development and design. Roger sincerely hopes to soon live in a world where people of all ages will be given the knowledge and opportunity to experience the joy of building their own games.

I would like to thank the people from Packt Publishing who helped me through the process of writing this book. And above all, my family, who lovingly accepted my, "Sorry, I can't do that, I'm writing a book" as an excuse to avoid every task and chore imaginable. (I wonder how long I can keep giving that excuse now that the book has been published...)

About the Reviewers

Fabio Cunha began web development about three years ago and worked as a mobile developer for two years. He currently works as a frontend developer in an e-learning company. He has his own blog (`http://www.fabiosistemas.com.br/blog/`) that describes all of the work that he does, and has published games on mobile platforms such as Android, iOS, and Blackberry.

> I would like to thank my mother, brother, and sister for always supporting me, my dad for teaching me to be a calmer person, and my girlfriend for always staying by my side.

Stelios Pallis is 25 years old and lives in Cyprus. He studied Computer Science at the University of Cyprus (UCY), and at the moment he is a postgraduate student there. In 2011, he started developing games, and as a fanatic gamer he loved developing games. In 2012, he founded a startup company called Gamethru, a company for developing mobiles games.

Gamethru has already published four mobile games; three are available in Google Play Store and one in App Store.

Marcio Valenzuela P is a biochemist who has studied programming as a hobby for over 12 years. He is perseverant, autodidactic, and is always looking into the latest technologies. Marcio started by picking up ASP back in the early 90's as Chief Web Developer for a consulting firm that developed web applications for private companies. He also delved into PHP applications with a MySQL database backend. Then, in 2008, he started on his path down iOS and has had experience in developing applications and games for the platform. His experience is mostly in business applications where there exists a cloud-based web service to interact with, and more recently, in games created in Cocos2d.

Marcio is the co-founder of `Activasolutions.com` and currently runs a small iOS project called `Santiapps.com`, which programs for companies wishing to enter the iOS platform. Marcio is a forum moderator at `RayWenderlich.com`.

I would like to acknowledge the time I have taken from raising my son to dedicate to this book. I just hope that someday Santiago follows in the programming tradition as it fosters critical skills such as problem-solving and innovation, which is something we share.

www.PacktPub.com

Support files, eBooks, discount offers and more

You might want to visit www.PacktPub.com for support files and downloads related to your book.

Did you know that Packt offers eBook versions of every book published, with PDF and ePub files available? You can upgrade to the eBook version at www.PacktPub.com and as a print book customer, you are entitled to a discount on the eBook copy. Get in touch with us at service@packtpub.com for more details.

At www.PacktPub.com, you can also read a collection of free technical articles, sign up for a range of free newsletters and receive exclusive discounts and offers on Packt books and eBooks.

http://PacktLib.PacktPub.com

Do you need instant solutions to your IT questions? PacktLib is Packt's online digital book library. Here, you can access, read and search across Packt's entire library of books.

Why Subscribe?

- ◆ Fully searchable across every book published by Packt
- ◆ Copy and paste, print and bookmark content
- ◆ On demand and accessible via web browser

Free Access for Packt account holders

If you have an account with Packt at www.PacktPub.com, you can use this to access PacktLib today and view nine entirely free books. Simply use your login credentials for immediate access.

Table of Contents

Preface

Cocos2d-x combines the benefits of using one of the most popular and test-proven 2D game frameworks out there with the power and portability of C++. So you get the best deal possible. Not only is the framework built to be easy to use and quick to implement, but it also allows your code to target more than one system.

This book shows you how to use the framework to quickly implement your ideas, and let Cocos2d-x help you with the translation of all that OpenGL gobbledygook, leaving you with all the fun parts, such as making sprites jump around and hit each other!

There are six examples of games in this book, two of them being physics-based games using Box2D. With each example, you'll learn more about the framework and the magical lines that can quickly add particle effects, animations, sounds, UI elements, and all sorts of wonderful things to your games.

Not only that, you will also learn how to target both iOS and Android devices, and how to cater for multiple screen sizes.

What this book covers

Chapter 1, *Installation*, guides you through the download and installation of the Cocos2d-x framework. It also examines the ins and outs of a basic Cocos2d-x application.

Chapter 2, *You plus C++ plus Cocos2d-x*, explains the main elements in the framework. It also covers the differences in syntax when developing in C++, and the differences in memory management when developing with Cocos2d-x.

Chapter 3, *Your First Game – Air Hockey*, kick-starts our game development tutorials by using Cocos2d-x to build an Air Hockey game. You learn how to load images for your sprites, how to display text, how to manage touches, and how to add sounds to your game.

Chapter 4, Fun with Sprites – Sky Defense, demonstrates the power of actions in Cocos2d-x, and shows how an entire game could be built with them. It also introduces the concept of sprite sheets and the steps required to build a universal app targeting different screen resolutions.

Chapter 5, On the Line – Rocket Through, adds two new elements to our game development tool box: how to draw primitives such as lines, curves, and circles; and how to use particle systems to improve the look of our game through the use of special effects.

Chapter 6, Quick and Easy Sprite – Victorian Rush Hour, shows how you can use Cocos2d-x to quickly implement game ideas for further testing and development by rapidly building game prototypes with place-holder sprites. In the game example used for this chapter, you'll also learn how to build a side-scrolling platform game.

Chapter 7, Adding the Looks – Victorian Rush Hour, continues with the project from the previous chapter, adding the final touches to the game, including a menu and a playable tutorial.

Chapter 8, Getting Physical – Box2D, introduces the popular Box2D API for physics simulations, guiding you through the process of using Box2D in the development of a pool game. You learn how to create bodies and manage the way they interact with each other.

Chapter 9, The Last Game – Eskimo, teaches you how to load external data for game levels, how to store game-related data locally, and how to structure your games with multiple scenes. We use a second Box2D game to illustrate these topics, plus a couple of new concepts, such as using notifications in your game.

Chapter 10, Code Once. Retire., guides you through the process of using Cocos2d-x to build an Android project and a hybrid project, targeting both iOS and Android. It teaches how to set up your development environment and the best practices for multi-target development.

What you need for this book

In order to run the games developed in this book on Apple devices, you will need Xcode and a Mac. Although the tutorials describe the development process using Xcode, in the last chapter of the book, you will also learn how the code can be compiled for Android devices, by using Eclipse.

Who this book is for

If you have a passion for games, then this book is for you. You may have used Cocos2d already (the Objective-C version of the framework) and are eager to learn its C++ ported version. Or you know a little bit of some other C-based language like Java, PHP, or Objective-C, and you want to learn how to develop 2D games in C++. Or you are a C++ developer already and want to know what's all the hoopla with Cocos2d-x. If you fit any of these scenarios, welcome aboard!

Conventions

In this book, you will find several headings appearing frequently.

To give clear instructions of how to complete a procedure or task, we use:

Time for action – heading

1. Action 1
2. Action 2
3. Action 3

Instructions often need some extra explanation so that they make sense, so they are followed with:

What just happened?

This heading explains the working of tasks or instructions that you have just completed.

You will also find some other learning aids in the book, including:

Pop quiz – heading

These are short multiple-choice questions intended to help you test your own understanding.

Have a go hero – heading

These are practical challenges that give you ideas for experimenting with what you have learned.

You will also find a number of styles of text that distinguish between different kinds of information. Here are some examples of these styles, and an explanation of their meaning.

Code words in text, database table names, folder names, filenames, file extensions, pathnames, dummy URLs, user input, and Twitter handles are shown as follows: "To make a sprite invisible, you use the `setVisible(false)` command."

A block of code is set as follows:

```
CCScene* GameLayer::scene()
{
    // 'scene' is an autorelease object
    CCScene *scene = CCScene::create();

    GameLayer *layer = GameLayer::create();

    scene->addChild(layer);

    return scene;
}
```

When we wish to draw your attention to a particular part of a code block, the relevant lines or items are set in bold:

```
# * Fine Tuning
#
key_buffer = 16M
key_buffer_size = 32M
max_allowed_packet = 16M
thread_stack = 512K
thread_cache_size = 8
max_connections = 300
```

Any command-line input or output is written as follows:

```
sudo ./install-templates-xcode.sh -u
```

New terms and **important words** are shown in bold. Words that you see on the screen, in menus or dialog boxes for example, appear in the text like this: " In the dialog box, select **cocos2d-x** under the **iOS** menu, and then choose the **cocos2dx** template. Hit **Next**.".

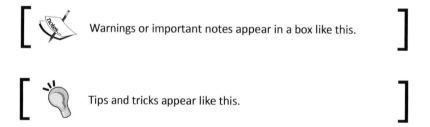

Warnings or important notes appear in a box like this.

Tips and tricks appear like this.

Reader feedback

Feedback from our readers is always welcome. Let us know what you think about this book—what you liked or may have disliked. Reader feedback is important for us to develop titles that you really get the most out of.

To send us general feedback, simply send an e-mail to feedback@packtpub.com, and mention the book title through the subject of your message.

If there is a topic that you have expertise in and you are interested in either writing or contributing to a book, see our author guide on www.packtpub.com/authors.

Customer support

Now that you are the proud owner of a Packt book, we have a number of things to help you to get the most from your purchase.

Downloading the example code

You can download the example code files for all Packt books you have purchased from your account at http://www.packtpub.com. If you purchased this book elsewhere, you can visit http://www.packtpub.com/support and register to have the files e-mailed directly to you.

Errata

Although we have taken every care to ensure the accuracy of our content, mistakes do happen. If you find a mistake in one of our books—maybe a mistake in the text or the code—we would be grateful if you would report this to us. By doing so, you can save other readers from frustration and help us improve subsequent versions of this book. If you find any errata, please report them by visiting http://www.packtpub.com/submit-errata, selecting your book, clicking on the **errata submission form** link, and entering the details of your errata. Once your errata are verified, your submission will be accepted and the errata will be uploaded to our website, or added to any list of existing errata, under the Errata section of that title.

Piracy

Piracy of copyright material on the Internet is an ongoing problem across all media. At Packt, we take the protection of our copyright and licenses very seriously. If you come across any illegal copies of our works, in any form, on the Internet, please provide us with the location address or website name immediately so that we can pursue a remedy.

Please contact us at copyright@packtpub.com with a link to the suspected pirated material.

We appreciate your help in protecting our authors, and our ability to bring you valuable content.

Questions

You can contact us at questions@packtpub.com if you are having a problem with any aspect of the book, and we will do our best to address it.

1
Installation

In this chapter we'll get things up and running on your machine so you can get the most out of the examples in this book. This will include information on downloading the framework and installing its templates, as well as an overview of the basic structure of a Cocos2d-x application.

I will also point you to some extra tools you could get to help you with the development process: tools to build sprite sheets, particle effects, and bitmap fonts. Although these tools are optional, and you can still learn how to work with sprite sheets, particles and bitmap fonts by following the examples given in this book, you might consider these tools for your own projects.

Things you will learn in this first chapter:

- ◆ How to download and install Cocos2d-x templates
- ◆ How to run your first application
- ◆ What the basic template looks like and how to find your way around it
- ◆ How to run the test samples that comes bundled with Cocos2d-x

Download and installation

All the examples in this book were developed on a Mac using Xcode. Although you can use Cocos2d-x to develop your games for other platforms, using different systems, the examples will focus on iOS and Mac. In *Chapter 10, Code Once. Retire.* I'll show you how to develop Android games with Cocos2d-x using the Eclipse IDE. But for now, I'll assume you are using a Mac and Xcode.

Xcode is free and can be downloaded from the Mac App store (`https://developer.apple.com/xcode/index.php`), but in order to test your code on an iOS device and publish your games, you will need a developer account with Apple, which will cost you USD 99 a year. You can find more information on their website: `https://developer.apple.com/`

So, assuming you have an internet connection, and that Xcode is ready to rock, let's begin!

Time for action – downloading and installing Cocos2d-x

We start by downloading the framework:

1. Go to `http://download.cocos2d-x.org/` and download the latest stable version of Cocos2d-x. For this book I'll be using version Cocos2d-2.0-x-2.0.4, which means the 2.0.4 C++ port of version 2.0 of Cocos2d.

2. Uncompress the files somewhere on your machine.

3. Open Terminal and type `cd` (that is `cd` and a space).

4. Drag the uncompressed folder you just downloaded to the **Terminal** window. You should see the path to the folder added to the command line. Hit *return* to go to that folder in **Terminal**.

5. Now type:

```
sudo ./install-templates-xcode.sh -u
```

6. Hit *return* again and you're done.

What just happened?

You have successfully installed the Cocos2d-x templates in your machine. With these in place, you can select the type of Cocos2d-x application you wish to build inside Xcode, and the templates will take care of copying all the necessary files into your application.

Next, open Xcode and select **Create a new Xcode Project**. You should see something like this:

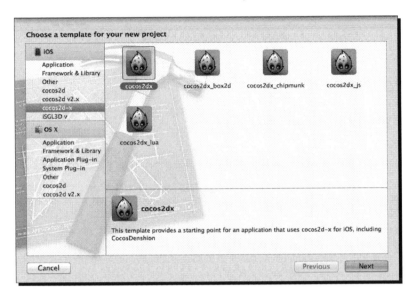

So let's build our first application.

Hello-x World-x

Let's create that old chestnut in computer programming: the hello world example.

Time for action – creating an application

Open **Xcode** and select **File | New | Project...** and follow these steps:

1. In the dialogue box select **cocos2d-x** under the **iOS** menu and choose the `cocos2dx` template. Hit **Next**.

2. Give the application a name, but not `HelloWorld`. I'll show you why in a second. You will be then asked to select a place to save the project and you are done.

3. Once your application is ready, click **Run** to build it. After that, this is what you should see in the simulator:

 When you run a **cocos2d-x** application in Xcode it is quite common for the program to post some warnings regarding your code, or most likely the frameworks. These will mostly reference deprecated methods, or statements that do not precisely follow more recent, and stricter rules of the current SDK. But that's okay. These warnings, though certainly annoying, can be ignored.

What just happened?

You created your first **Cocos2d-x** application using the cocos2dx template, sometimes referred to as the basic template.

The other template options include one with Box2D, one with Chipmunk (both related to physics simulation), one with JavaScript, and one with Lua.

The last two options allow you to code some or all of your game using those script languages instead of the native C++; and they work just as you would expect a scripting language to work, meaning the commands written in either Javascript or Lua are actually replaced and interpreted as C++ commands by the compiler.

Now if you look at the files created by the basic template you will see a HelloWorldScene class file. That's the reason I didn't want you to call your application HelloWorld, because I didn't want you to have the impression that the file name was based on your project name. It isn't. You will always get a HelloWorldScene file unless you change the template itself.

Now let's go over the sample application and its files:

The folder structure

First you have the `Resources` folder, where you find the images used by the application.

The `ios` folder has the necessary underlying connections between your app and iOS. For other platforms, you will have their necessary linkage files in separate folders targeting their respective platform (like an `android` folder the Android platform, for instance.)

In the `libs` folder you have all the `cocos2dx` files, plus `CocosDenshion` files (for sound support) and a bunch of other extensions. Using a different template for your projects will result in a different folder structure here, based on what needs to be added to your project. So you will see a `Box2D` folder, for example, if you choose the Box2D template.

In the `Classes` folder you have your application. In here, everything is written in C++ and this is the home for the part of your code that will hopefully not need to change, however many platforms you target with your application.

Now let us go over the main classes of the basic application.

The iOS linkage classes

AppController and RootViewController are responsible for setting up OpenGL in iOS as well as telling the underlying operating system that your application is about to say Hello... To the World.

These classes are written with a mix of Objective-C and C++, as all the nice brackets and the .mm extensions show. You will change very little if anything in these classes; and again that will reflect in changes to the way iOS handles your application. So other targets would require the same instructions or none at all depending on the target.

In AppController for instance, I could add support for multitouch. And in RootViewController, I could limit the screen orientations supported by my application.

The AppDelegate class

This class marks the first time your C++ app will talk to the underlying OS. It attempts to map the main events that mobile devices wants to dispatch and listen to. From here on, all your application will be written in C++ (unless you need something else).

In AppDelegate you should setup CCDirector (the cocos2d-x all powerful singleton manager object) to run your application just the way you want. You can:

- Get rid of the application status information
- Change the frame rate of your application
- Tell CCDirector where your high definition images are, and where your standard definition images are, as well as which to use
- You can change the overall scale of your application to suit different screens
- The AppDelegate class is also the best place to start any preloading process
- And, most importantly, it is here you tell the CCDirector object what CCScene to begin your application with

Here too you will handle what happens to your application if the OS decides to kill it, push it aside, or hang it upside down to dry. All you need to do is place your logic inside the correct event handler: applicationDidEnterBackground or applicationWillEnterForeground.

The HelloWorldScene class

When you run the application you get a screen with the words Hello World and a bunch of numbers in one corner. These are the display stats you decided you wanted around in the AppDelegate class.

The actual screen is created by the oddly named `HelloWorldScene` class. It is a `Layer` class that creates its own scene (don't worry if you don't know what a `Layer` class is, or a `Scene` class, you will soon enough).

When it initializes, `HelloWorldScene` puts a button on screen that you can press to exit the application. The button is actually a Menu item, part of a Menu group consisting of one button, two image states for that button, and one callback event, triggered when the said button is pressed.

The Menu group automatically handles touch events targeting its members, so you don't get to see any of that code floating about.

There is also the necessary `Label` object to show the `Hello World` message and the background image.

Who begets whom

If you never worked with either Cocos2d or Cocos2d-x before, the way the initial `scene()` method is instantiated may lead to dizziness. To recap, in `AppDelegate` you have:

```
CCScene *pScene = HelloWorld::scene();
pDirector->runWithScene(pScene);
```

`CCDirector` needs a `CCScene` object to run, which you can think of as being your application, basically. `CCScene` needs something to show, which in this case is a `CCLayer` class. `CCScene` is then said to contain a `CCLayer` class.

Here a `CCScene` object is created through a static method `scene` inside a `CCLayer` derived class. So the layer creates the scene, and the scene immediately adds the layer to itself. Huh?

Relax. This incestuous-like instantiation will most likely only happen once, and you have nothing to do with it when it happens. So you can easily ignore all these funny goings-on and look the other way. I promise instantiations will be much easier after this first one.

Further information

Follow these steps to access one of the best sources for reference material on Cocos2d-x: its `Test` project.

Time for action – running the test samples

You open the test project just like you would do for any other Xcode project:

1. Go inside the folder you downloaded for the framework, and navigate to `samples/TestCpp/proj.ios/TestCpp.xcodeproj`.

2. Open that project in Xcode. When you run the project, you will see inside the simulator a long list of tests, all nicely organized by topic. Pick any one to review.

3. Better yet, navigate to `samples/TestCpp/Classes` and if you have a program like `TextWrangler` or some equivalent, you can open that entire directory inside a **Disk Browser** window and have all that information ready for referencing right at your desktop.

What just happened?

With the test samples you can visualize most features in Cocos2d-x and see what they do, as well as some of the ways you can initialize and customize them.

I will refer to the code found in the tests quite often. As usual with programming, there is always a different way to accomplish a given task, so sometimes after showing you one way, I'll refer to another one that you can find (and by then easily understand) inside the Test classes.

The other tools

Now comes the part where you may need to spend a bit more money to get some extremely helpful tools. In this book's examples I use four of them:

1. A tool to help build sprite sheets: I'll use **Texture Packer** (`http://www.codeandweb.com/texturepacker`). There are other alternatives, like **Zwoptex** (`http://zwopple.com/zwoptex/`). And they usually offer some features for free.

2. A tool to help build particle effects: I'll use **Particle Designer** (`http://www.71squared.com/en/particledesigner`). Depending on your operating system you may find free tools online for this. Cocos2d-x comes bundled with some common particle effects that you can customize. But to do it blindly is a process I do not recommend.

3. A tool to help build bitmap fonts: I'll use **Glyph Designer** (http://www.71squared.com/en/glyphdesigner). But there are others: **bmGlyph** (which is not as expensive), **FontBuilder** (which is free). It is not extremely hard to build a Bitmap font by hand, not nearly as hard as building a particle effect from scratch, but doing it once is enough to convince you to get one of these tools fast.

4. A tool to produce sound effects: No contest. **cfxr** for Mac or the original **sfxr** for Windows. Both are free (http://www.drpetter.se/project_sfxr.html and http://thirdcog.eu/apps/cfxr respectively).

Summary

You just learned how to install Cocos2d-x templates and create a basic application. You also learned enough of the structure of a basic Cocos2d-x application to get started on building your first game.

Keep the Test classes by your side as you go over the examples in this book and you will be a Cocos2d-x pro in no time.

But first, let's go over a few things regarding the framework and its native language.

2

You plus C++ plus Cocos2d-x

This chapter will be aimed at two types of developers: the original Cocos2d developer who is scared of C++ but won't admit it to his friends; and the C++ coder who never even heard of Cocos2d and finds Objective-C funny looking.

I'll go over the main syntax differences Objective-C developers should pay attention to, and the few code style changes involved in developing with Cocos2d-x that C++ developers should be aware of.

But first, a quick introduction to Cocos2d-x and what it is all about.

You will learn:

◆ What is Cocos2d-x and what it can do for you

◆ How to create classes in C++

◆ How to memory manage your objects in Cocos2d-x and C++

◆ What you can get out of CCObject

Cocos2d-x – an introduction

So what is a 2D framework? If I had to define it in as few words as possible, I'd say: rectangles in a loop.

At the heart of Cocos2d-x you find the **sprite** (known as CCSprite) and what that class does, in simple terms, is to keep a reference to two very important rectangles. One is the image (or texture) rectangle, also called the source rectangle, and one is the destination rectangle. If you want an image to appear at the center of the screen, you will use CCSprite. You will pass it information on what and where that image source is, and where on the screen you want it to appear.

There is not much that needs to be done to the source rectangle, but there's loads that can be changed in the destination rectangle, including its position on the screen, its size, opacity, rotation and so on.

Cocos2d-x then will take care of all the OpenGL drawing necessary to display your image where you want it and how you want it, and it will do so inside a render loop. Your code will most likely tap into that same loop to update its own logic.

Pretty much any 2D game you can think of can be built with Cocos2d-x with just a few sprites and a loop.

The containers

Also important in Cocos2d-x is the notion of containers (or nodes). These are all the objects that can have sprites (or other nodes) inside them. This is extremely useful at times because by changing aspects of a given container, you automatically change aspects of its children. Move the container and all its children will move with it. Rotate the container and well, you get the picture.

The containers are: CCScene, CCLayer, and CCSprite. They all inherit from a base container class called CCNode. Each container has its peculiarities, but basically you will arrange them as follows:

- ◆ CCScene: It will contain one or more CCLayer. It is common to break applications into multiple scenes; for instance, one for the main menu, one for settings, and one for the actual game. Technically each scene will behave as a separate entity in your application, almost as sub-applications themselves, and you can run a series of transition effects when changing between scenes.

- ◆ CCLayer: It will most likely contain CCSprite. There are a number of specialized CCLayer objects, aimed at saving you, the developer, some time in creating things such as menus (CCMenu) or colored backgrounds (CCLayerColor). You can have more than one CCLayer per scene, but good planning usually makes this unnecessary. CCLayer is often thought of as a CCNode that listens to user input events (such as touch, accelerometer, and gyroscope) since it comes bundled with all the protocols necessary for that.

- ◆ CCSprite: These contain your images and will be added to CCLayer derived containers. To my mind this is the most important class in all of Cocos2d-x. So much so that after your application initializes, when both a CCScene and a CCLayer are created, you could build your entire game only with CCSprites and never use another container class in Cocos2d-x.

◆ CCNode: This superclass to all containers blurs the line between itself and CCLayer, and even CCSprite at times. It has its own set of specialized subclasses (besides the ones already mentioned), like CCMotionStreak, CCParallaxNode, and CCSpriteBatchNode, to name a few. With a few adjustments, it can behave just as CCLayer. But most of the time you will use it to create your own specialized nodes or as a general reference in polymorphism.

The director and caches

Then comes the all-knowing CCDirector and all-encompassing cache objects. CCDirector manages scenes and knows all about your application. You will make calls to it to get to that information, and to change some of it: things such as screen size, frame rate, scale factor, and so on.

The caches are **collector objects**. The most important ones are CCTextureCache, CCSpriteFrameCache, and CCAnimationCache. These are responsible for storing key information regarding those two important rectangles I talked about. In fact, every sort of data that is used repeatedly in Cocos2d-x will be kept in some sort of cache list.

Both CCDirector and all cache objects are **singletons**: a special sort of class that is instantiated only once and this one instance can usually be accessed by any other object.

Then there is all the other stuff

After the basic containers, the caches and the director, comes the other 90 percent of the framework. Among all this extra goodness, you will find:

◆ CCActions: Animations will be handled through these, and what a treat they are.

◆ CCParticles: Particle systems for your delight.

◆ Specialized CCNodes: For things like menus, progress bars, special effects, parallax effect, tile maps, and much, much more.

◆ The **macros, structures, and helper** methods: Hundreds of time-saving, magical bits of logic. You don't need to know them all, but chances are you will be coding something that can be easily replaced by a macro or helper method and will feel incredibly silly when you find out about it later.

But you don't know C++?

Don't worry. The C part is easy, the first plus goes by really fast, but that second plus, Oh, boy.

Remember, it is C. And if you have coded in Objective-C, with the original Cocos2d, you know good old C already, even if you saw it in between brackets most of the time.

But C++ also has classes just like Objective-C, and these classes are declared in the interface files just like in Objective-C. So let's go over the creation of a C++ class.

The interface

This will be done in a .h file. We'll use a text editor to create this file since I don't want any code hinting and auto-completion features getting in the way of you learning the basics of C++ syntax. So for now at least, open up your favorite text editor and let's create a class interface.

Time for action – creating the interface

The interface, or header file, is just a text file with the .h extension:

1. Create a new text file and save it as `HelloWorld.h`. Then enter these lines at the top:

    ```
    #ifndef __HELLOWORLD_H__
    #define __HELLOWORLD_H__
    #include "cocos2d.h"
    ```

2. Next add the namespace declaration:

    ```
    using namespace cocos2d;
    ```

3. Then declare your class name, and the name of any inherited classes:

    ```
    class HelloWorld : public cocos2d::CCLayer {
    ```

4. Next we add the properties and methods:

    ```
    protected:
    int _score;

    public:

        HelloWorld();
        ~HelloWorld();

        virtual bool init();
        static cocos2d::CCScene* scene();
        void update(float dt);
        inline int addTwoIntegers (int one, int two) {
            return one + two;
        }
    };
    ```

5. We finish by closing the `#ifndef` statement:

    ```
    #endif // __HELLOWORLD_H__
    ```

What just happened?

You created a header file in C++. Let's go over the important bits of information:

- In C++ you `include`, you do not `import`. The `import` statement in Objective-C checks to see if something needs to be included; `include` does not. But we accomplish the same thing through that clever use of definitions at the top. There are other ways to run the same check (with `#pragma once`, for instance) but this one is added to any new C++ files you create in Xcode.

- You can make your life easier by declaring the namespaces you'll use in the class. These are similar to packages in some languages. You may have noticed that all the uses of `cocos2d::` in the code is not necessary because of the namespace declaration. But I wanted to show you the bit you can get rid of by adding a namespace declaration.

- So next you give your class a name and you may choose to inherit from some other class. In C++ you can have as many superclasses as you want. And you must declare if your super is public or not.

- You declare your `public`, `protected` and `private` methods and members between the curly braces. `HelloWorld` is the constructor and `~HelloWorld` is the destructor (it will do what `dealloc` does in Objective-C).

- The `virtual` keyword is related to overrides. When you mark a method as virtual you are telling the compiler not to set in stone whom the method belongs to, but to keep it in memory until execution reveals the obvious owner. Otherwise the compiler may decide erroneously a method belongs to the super and not its inheriting class. You only need use the keyword once in the superclass to mark potential overrides, but it is common practice to repeat the `virtual` keyword in all subclasses so developers know which methods are overrides. In this case `init` comes from `CCLayer` and `HelloWorld` wants to override it:

    ```
    virtual bool init();
    ```

- Oh, yes: in C++ you must declare overrides in your interfaces. No exception.

- The inline methods are something new to you, probably. These methods are added to the code by the compiler wherever they are called for. So every time I make a call to `addTwoIntegers`, the compiler will replace it with the lines for the method declared in the interface. Therefore, the inline methods work just as statements inside a method, and do not require their own bit of memory in the stack; however, if you call a two-line inline method 50 times in your program, the compiler will add hundred lines to your code.

The implementation

This will be done in a .cpp file. Let's go back to our text editor and create the implementation for our HelloWorld class.

Time for action – creating the implementation

The implementation is a text file with the .cpp extension:

1. Create a new text file and save it as HelloWorld.cpp. At the top let's start by including our header file:

```
#include "HelloWorld.h"
```

2. Next we implement our constructor and destructor:

```
HelloWorld::HelloWorld () {
    //constructor
}

HelloWorld::~HelloWorld () {
    //destructor
}
```

3. Then comes our static method:

```
CCScene* HelloWorld::scene() {
    CCScene *scene = CCScene::create();

    HelloWorld *layer = HelloWorld::create();

    scene->addChild(layer);

    return scene;
}
```

4. And our two remaining public methods:

```
bool HelloWorld::init() {
    // call to super
    if ( !CCLayer::init() )
    {
        return false;
    }

    //create main loop
    this->schedule(schedule_selector(HelloWorld::update));
```

```
        return true;
    }

    void HelloWorld::update (float dt) {
        //the main loop
    }
```

What just happened?

We created the implementation for our `HelloWorld` class. Here are the most important things to notice:

- The `HelloWorld::` scope resolution is not optional here. Every single method declared in your interface to belong to the new class needs the correct scope resolution in the implementation file.

- You also need the scope resolution when calling the superclass, for example `CCLayer::init()`. There is no built-in `super` keyword in the standard C++ library.

- You use `this` instead of `self`. The `->` notation is used to access public methods inside an object, and the `.` (dot) notation is used for public properties.

- There is a different macro for each type of selector you may need in your code (in the previous example there is a `schedule_selector` macro), these macros are provided by the framework. Selectors are ways to pass callbacks to other objects.

- The inline methods are not, of course, implemented in the .cpp file since they exist only in the interface.

That's enough of the syntax for now. C++ is one of the most extensive languages out there and I do not wish to leave you with the impression I have covered all of it. But it is a language made by developers for developers. Trust me, you will feel right at home working with it.

The information listed previously will become even clearer once we move on to building the games. But now, onwards to the big scary monster: memory management.

Instantiation and memory management

There is no **Automatic Reference Counting (ARC)** in Cocos2d-x, so Objective-C developers who have forgotten memory management might have a problem here.

The rule regarding memory management with C++ is very simple: if you `new`, you must `delete`. Cocos2d-x, however, will add a few other options and commands, similar to the ones we have in Objective-C (without ARC). That is because Cocos2d-x, unlike C++, and very much like Objective-C, has a root class. The framework is more than just a C++ port of Cocos2d. It also ports certain notions of Objective-C to C++, in order to recreate its memory management system.

Cocos2d-x has a CCObject class which is the root of every major object in the framework. It allows the framework to have autorelease pools, and retain counts, as well other Objective-C equivalents.

When instantiating Cocos2d-x objects you basically have two options.

Option 1 – use static methods

This is the recommended way. The three-stage instantiation process of Objective-C, with alloc, init, and autorelease/retain is recreated here. So for instance a Player class, which extends CCSprite, might have the following methods:

```
Player::Player () {
    this->setPosition  ( ccp(0,0) );
}

Player * Player::create () {

    Player * player = new Player();

    if (player && player->initWithSpriteFrameName("player.png")) {
        player->autorelease();
        return player;
    }
    CC_SAFE_DELETE(player);
    return NULL;
}
```

For instantiation, you call the static create method. It will create a new Player object as an empty husk version of Player. No major initialization should happen inside the constructor, just in case you may have to delete the object due to some failure in the instantiation process. Cocos2d-x has a series of macros for object deletion and release, like the CC_SAFE_DELETE used previously.

You then initialize the super through one of its available methods. In Cocos2d-x these init methods return a boolean value for success. You may now begin filling the Player object with some data.

If successful, then init your object with its proper data, if not done in the previous step, and return it as an autorelease object.

So in your code the object would be instantiated like this:

```
Player * player = Player::create();
this->addChild(player);//this will retain the object
```

Even if the variable player were a member of the class (say, m_player), you wouldn't have to retain it to keep it in scope. By adding the object to some Cocos2d-x list or cache the object is automatically retained, so you may continue to address that memory through its pointer.

```
m_player = Player::create();
this->addChild(m_player);//this will retain the object
//m_player still references the memory address
//but does not need to be released or deleted by you
```

Option 2 – C++, Cocos2d-x style

In this option you would instantiate the previous Player object like this:

```
Player * player = new Player();
player->initWithSpriteFrameName("player.png");
this->addChild(player);
player->autorelease();
```

Player could do without a static method in this case and the *player pointer will not access the same memory in future as it's set to be autoreleased (so it would not stick around for long). The memory would not leak, however, in this case. It would still be retained by a Cocos2d-x list (the addChild command takes care of that). You can still access that memory by going over the list of children added to this.

If you needed the pointer to be a member property you could use retain() instead of autorelease():

```
m_player = new Player();
m_player->initWithSpriteFrameName("player.png");
this->addChild(m_player);
m_player->retain();
```

Then sometime later you would have to release it, otherwise it would leak:

```
m_player->release();
```

Hardcore C++ developers may choose to forget all about the autorelease pool and simply attempt to use new and delete:

```
Player * player = new Player();
player->initWithSpriteFrameName("player.png");
this->addChild(player);
delete player;//This will crash!
```

This will not work. You have to use autorelease, retain, or leave the previous code without the delete command and hope there won't be any leak.

C++ developers must be aware that CCObjects are managed by the framework. This means that objects are being added to caches and the autorelease pool internally, even though you may not want this to happen. When you create that Player sprite, for instance, the player.png file you used will be added to the texture cache, or the sprite frame cache. When you add the sprite to a layer, the sprite will be added to a list of all children of that layer, and this list will be managed by the framework. My advice is, relax, and let the framework work for you.

Non-C++ developers should be aware that any class not derived from CCObject should be managed the usual way: if you are creating a new object you must delete it at some point.

```
MyObject * object = new MyObject();
delete object;
```

What you get with CCObject

With CCObject you get managed objects, as I said, plus some Objective-C equivalents that Objective-C developers may find hard to do without when moving to Cocos2d-x.

Cocos2d-x comes with a CCArray collection object that combines features from both NSArray and NSMutableArray. It can only store the CCObject derived objects, however; ditto for its CCDictionary and its similarity to NSDictionary and NSMutableDictionary from Objective-C.

There is a CCString wrapper for both the const char* and std::string elements, with methods similar to the ones you find in NSString.

There is a CCInteger wrapper for integers, so you can store integers in a CCArray object. And even a CCSet class for fast iterations similar to NSSet.

Once again, every CCObject derived class can be managed the way things used to be managed in Objective-C before ARC.

C++ does come packed with its own wonderful dynamic list classes, similar to the ones you would find in Java and C#. But for CCObject derived objects, you would probably be best served by Cocos2d-x managed lists.

In the examples that follow in this book I will code primarily from within the framework, so you will get to see plenty of examples of CCArray being used, for instance, but I will also use a vector or two in some of the games.

Summary

Hopefully non-C++ developers have now learned there is nothing to be feared from the language; and hardcore C++ developers have not scoffed too much at the notion of a root class and its retains and autoreleases.

All the stuff root classes have brought to languages such as Java and Objective-C will forever be a moot point. The creepy, underlying operations that go on behind your back with root objects cannot be shut down or controlled. They are not optional. And this forceful nature of root objects has bothered C++ developers ever since notions like garbage collectors first surfaced.

Having said that, memory management of `CCObjects` is extremely helpful and I hope even the most distrustful developers will soon learn to be thankful for it.

And, furthermore, Cocos2d-x is awesome!

So let's create a game already.

3
Your First Game – Air Hockey

We are going to build an Air Hockey game that will introduce you to all the main aspects of building a project with Cocos2d-x. These include: setting up the project's configuration, loading images, loading sounds, building a game for more than one screen resolution, and managing touch events.

Oh, and you will need to call a friend. This is a two player game. Go on, I'll wait here.

By the end of this chapter you will know:

- ◆ How to build an iPad-only game
- ◆ How to enable multi-touch
- ◆ How to support both retina and non-retina displays
- ◆ How to load images and sounds
- ◆ How to play sound effects
- ◆ How to create sprites
- ◆ How to extend the Cocos2d-x CCSprite class
- ◆ How to create labels and update them

Without further ado...

Game configurations

The game will have the following characteristics:

- It must support multi-touch since it's a two player game
- It must be played on large screens since it's a two player game
- It must support retina displays because we want to cash in on that
- It must be played only in portrait mode because I built the art in portrait

So let's create our project.

Time for action – creating your game project

From here on we'll use Xcode to create and manage all our projects.

1. Open Xcode and create a new project with the Cocos2d-x basic template.
2. Call it `Air Hockey`, and set its **Device Family** to **iPad**.
3. Save it and please remember where you saved it. We will need to navigate to this folder in a moment.

What just happened?

You created a project from the basic template, targeting iPads, and you are ready to set it up with the rest of the configurations I described earlier.

Let's do that now.

Time for action – laying down the rules

We'll update the `AppController.mm` and `RootViewController.mm` files:

1. Go to `AppController.mm` and inside the `(BOOL) application:(UIApplication *)application didFinishLaunchingWithOptions:(NSDictionary *)launchOptions` method below the section where the `EAGLView *__glView` object is instantiated, write this line:

   ```
   [__glView setMultipleTouchEnabled:YES];
   ```

2. Now go to `RootViewController.mm` and look for the `shouldAutorotateToInterfaceOrientation` method. Change the line inside the method to read:

   ```
   return UIInterfaceOrientationIsPortrait( interfaceOrientation );
   ```

3. Finally, a few lines below in the `supportedInterfaceOrientations` method change the line inside the conditional to:

```
return UIInterfaceOrientationMaskPortrait;
```

What just happened?

We just told `AppController` we want to support multi-touch. And we told `RootViewController` we want our application to play in either of the two supported portrait modes.

Supporting retina displays

Now let's add the images to our project.

Time for action – adding the image files

First, we download the images for this project, then we add them in Xcode:

1. Go to this book's support page (`www.packtpub.com/support`) and download the `7341_03_RESOURCES.zip` file. Inside it you should find two folders, one called `hd` and another called `sd`.

2. Go to your `Project` folder, the actual folder in your system. Drag the `hd` folder and the `sd` folder to the `Resources` folder inside your project.

3. Go back to Xcode. Select the `Resources` folder in your project navigation panel. Then go to **File | Add Files** to `Air Hockey`.

4. In the **File** window navigate to the `Resources` folder and select both the `sd` and `hd` folders.

5. This is very important: Make sure **Create folder references for any added folders** is selected. Also make sure you selected `Air Hockey` as the target. It wouldn't hurt to make sure **Copy items to destination...** is also selected.

6. Click **Add**.

What just happened?

You added the necessary image files for your `Air Hockey` game. These come in two versions, one for retina displays (high definition) and one for non-retina displays (standard definition). It is very important that references are added to the actual folders, only in this way will Xcode be able to have two files with the same name inside the project and still keep them apart; one in each folder.

Now let's tell Cocos2d-x where to look for the correct files.

Time for action – adding retina support

This time we'll work with the class `AppDelegate.cpp`:

1. Go to `AppDelegate.cpp`. Inside the `applicationDidFinishLaunching` method, and below the `pDirector->setOpenGLView( pEGLView)` line add these lines:

    ```
    CCSize screenSize = pEGLView->getFrameSize();
    CCEGLView::sharedOpenGLView()->setDesignResolutionSize(768, 1024,
    kResolutionExactFit);
    if (screenSize.width > 768) {
       CCFileUtils::sharedFileUtils()->setResourceDirectory("hd");
       pDirector->setContentScaleFactor(2);
    } else {
       CCFileUtils::sharedFileUtils()->setResourceDirectory("sd");
       pDirector->setContentScaleFactor(1);
    }
    ```

2. Save the file.

Downloading the example code

You can download the example code files for all Packt books you have purchased from your account at `http://www.packtpub.com`. If you purchased this book elsewhere, you can visit `http://www.packtpub.com/support` and register to have the files e-mailed directly to you.

What just happened?

An entire book could be written about this topic; although in this first example, we have a very simple implementation for supporting multiple screen sizes since we are only targeting iPads. Here we are saying: Hey, `AppDelegate`, I designed this game for a 768 x 1024 screen. All the values for positioning and font size were chosen for that screen size. If the screen is larger, make sure you grab the files from the `hd` folder and change the scale by which you will multiply all my positioning and font sizes. If the screen has the same size I designed the game for, use the files in the `sd` folder and set the scale to one.

`CCFileUtils` will look for every file you load for your game first inside `Resources | sd` (or `hd`). If it doesn't find them there, it will try to find them in `Resources`. This is a good thing because files shared by both versions only need adding to the project once, inside `Resources`. That is what we'll do now with the sound files.

Adding sound effects

This game has two files for sound effects. You will find them in the same zip file you downloaded previously.

Time for action – adding the sound files

Assuming you have the sound files from the downloaded resources, let's add them to the project:

1. Drag both the .wav files to the Resources folder inside your Project folder.

2. Then go to Xcode, select the Resources folder in the file navigation panel and select **File | Add Files to** Air Hockey.

3. Make sure the Air Hockey target is selected. Add the wav files.

4. Go to AppDelegate.cpp again. At the top, add this include:

   ```
   #include "SimpleAudioEngine.h"
   ```

5. Then below the USING_NS_CC macro (for using namespace cocos2d), add:

   ```
   using namespace CocosDenshion;
   ```

6. Then just below the lines you added in the previous section, inside applicationDidFinishLaunching, add these two gigantic lines:

   ```
   SimpleAudioEngine::sharedEngine()->preloadEffect(
   CCFileUtils::sharedFileUtils()->fullPathFromRelativePath("hit.
   wav") );
   SimpleAudioEngine::sharedEngine()->preloadEffect(
   CCFileUtils::sharedFileUtils()-
   >fullPathFromRelativePath("score.wav") );
   ```

What just happened?

With the preloadEffect method from CocosDenshion you have managed to preload the files, as well as instantiate and initialize SimpleAudioEngine. This step will always take a tow on your application's processing power, so it's best to do it early on.

By now, the folder structure for your game should look like this:

Extending CCSprite

No, there is nothing wrong with CCSprite. I just picked a game where we need a bit more information from some of its sprites. In this case we want to store where a sprite is and where it will be once the current iteration of the game is completed. We will also need a helper method to get the sprite's radius.

So let's create our GameSprite class.

Time for action – adding GameSprite.cpp

From here on, we'll create any new classes inside Xcode:

1. In Xcode, select the Classes folder and then go to **File | New | File** and inside the **iOS** tab select **C and C++** and then **C++ Class**.

2. Call it GameSprite.

3. Select the new GameSprite.h interface file and replace the code there with this:

```cpp
#ifndef __GAMESPRITE_H__
#define __GAMESPRITE_H__
#include "cocos2d.h"

using namespace cocos2d;

class GameSprite : public CCSprite {
public:

    CC_SYNTHESIZE(CCPoint, _nextPosition, NextPosition);
    CC_SYNTHESIZE(CCPoint, _vector, Vector);
    CC_SYNTHESIZE(CCTouch *, _touch, Touch);

    GameSprite(void);
    ~GameSprite(void);

    static GameSprite* gameSpriteWithFile(const char *
pszFileName);

    virtual void setPosition(const CCPoint& pos);
    float radius();

};
#endif // __GAMESPRITE_H__
```

What just happened?

In the interface we declare the class to be a subclass of the public CCSprite class.

Then we add three synthesized properties. In Cocos2d-x, these are macros for creating getters and setters. You declare the type, the protected variable name, and the words that will be appended to the get and set methods. So in the first CC_SYNTHESIZE method, a getNextPosition and setNextPosition method will be created to deal with the CCPoint value inside the _nextPosition protected variable.

We also add the constructor and destructor for our class, and the ubiquitous static method for instantiation. This receives as a parameter the image file name used by the sprite.

We finish off by overriding setPosition from CCSprite and adding the declaration for our helper method radius.

The next step then is to implement our new class.

Time for action – implementing GameSprite

With the header out of the way, all we need to do is implement our methods:

1. Select the GameSprite.cpp file and let's start on the instantiation logic of the class:

    ```cpp
    #include "GameSprite.h"

    GameSprite::GameSprite(void){
        _vector = ccp(0,0);
    }

    GameSprite::~GameSprite(void){
    }

    GameSprite* GameSprite::gameSpriteWithFile(const char *
    pszFileName) {
        GameSprite * sprite = new GameSprite();
        if (sprite && sprite->initWithFile(pszFileName)) {
            sprite->autorelease();
            return sprite;
        }
        CC_SAFE_DELETE(sprite);
        return NULL;
    }
    ```

2. Next we need to override the CCNode method setPosition. We need to make sure that whenever we change the position of the sprite the new value is also used by _nextPosition:

```
void GameSprite::setPosition(const CCPoint& pos) {
    CCSprite::setPosition(pos);
    if (!_nextPosition.equals(pos)) {
        _nextPosition = pos;
    }
}
```

3. And finally we implement our new method to retrieve the radius of our sprite, which we determine to be half the width of its texture:

```
float GameSprite::radius() {
    return getTexture()->getContentSize().width * 0.5f;
}
```

What just happened?

Things only begin happening in the static method. We create a new GameSprite class, then we call initWithFile on it. This is a GameSprite method inherited from its superclass; it returns a boolean value for success. The static method ends by returning an autorelease version of the GameSprite object.

The setPosition override makes sure _nextPosition receives the position information whenever the sprite is placed somewhere. And the helper radius method returns half of the sprite's texture width.

Have a go hero

Change the radius method to an inline method in the interface and remove it from the implementation file.

The actual game scene

Finally, we'll get to see all our work and have some fun with it. But first, let's rename the HelloWorldScene class. This is technically optional, but...

Rename the HelloWorldScene files to GameLayer, and the class inside them from HelloWorld to GameLayer. These are the names I'll use in the following steps; you can pick different ones if you'd wish, just make the appropriate adjustments to the code.

References to the class must be changed in two lines of `AppDelegate.cpp`, and also the `include` statement at the top of `HelloWorldScene.cpp`. Of course, any scope resolution changes (the `HelloWorld::` funny bits) must be changed in `HelloWorldScene.cpp` as well.

We'll start with the layer's interface.

Time for action – coding the GameLayer interface

`GameLayer` is the main container in our game and is coded as follows:

1. Select your `GameLayer.h`, then replace the code here with:

    ```
    #ifndef __GAMELAYER_H__
    #define __GAMELAYER_H__

    #define GOAL_WIDTH 400
    ```

    We define the width of the goals in pixels.

2. Next add the declarations for our sprites and our score text labels:

    ```
    #include "cocos2d.h"
    #include "GameSprite.h"

    using namespace cocos2d;

    class GameLayer : public cocos2d::CCLayer
    {
        GameSprite * _player1;
        GameSprite * _player2;
        GameSprite * _ball;

        CCArray * _players;
        CCLabelTTF * _player1ScoreLabel;
        CCLabelTTF * _player2ScoreLabel;
    ```

    We have the `GameSprite` objects for two players (the weird looking things called mallets), and the ball (called puck). We'll store the two players in `CCArray`. And we have two text labels to display score for each player.

3. Declare a variable to store the screen size. We'll use this a lot for positioning:

    ```
    CCSize _screenSize;
    ```

4. Add variables to store the score information and a method to update these scores on screen:

    ```
    int _player1Score;
    int _player2Score;

    void playerScore (int player);
    ```

5. Finally, let's add our methods:

```
public:

    ~GameLayer();

    virtual bool init();

    static CCScene* scene();

    CREATE_FUNC(GameLayer);

    virtual void ccTouchesBegan(CCSet* pTouches, CCEvent*
    event);
    virtual void ccTouchesMoved(CCSet* pTouches, CCEvent*
    event);
    virtual void ccTouchesEnded(CCSet* pTouches, CCEvent*
    event);
    void update (float dt);
};
#endif // __GAMELAYER_H__
```

There is a destructor method so we can release stuff, then the `CCLayer init` methods that came in with the template, and finally the overrides for the touch events (every `CCLayer` has them) and our loop method, called `update`. These touch event handlers will be added to our class to handle when users touches begin, when they move across the screen and when they end.

What just happened?

`GameLayer` is our game. It contains references to all the sprites we need to control and update, as well as all game data.

In the class implementation, all the logic starts inside the `init` method.

Time for action – implementing init()

Inside `init()` we'll build the game screen, bringing in all the sprites and labels we'll need for the game. So right after the `if` statement where we call the super `CCLayer::init` method, we add:

```
_player1Score = 0;
_player2Score = 0;
_screenSize = CCDirector::sharedDirector()->getWinSize();
```

1. We initialize the score values and grab the screen size from the all-knowing singleton CCDirector. We'll use the screen size to position all sprites relatively. Next, we create our first CCSprite. It is created with an image file name, which CCFileUtils will take care of loading from the correct folder:

```
CCSprite * court = CCSprite::create("court.png");
court->setPosition(ccp(_screenSize.width * 0.5, _screenSize.height
* 0.5));
this->addChild(court);
```

2. Get in the habit of positioning sprites with relative values, and not absolute ones, so we can support more screen sizes. And say hello to the macro ccp, used to create points; chances are that the this method you will use the most in Cocos2d-x.

3. We finish by adding the sprite as a child to our GameLayer (the court sprite does not need to be a GameSprite).

4. Next we use our spanking-new GameSprite class, carefully positioning the objects on screen:

```
_player1 = GameSprite::gameSpriteWithFile("mallet.png");
_player1->setPosition(ccp(_screenSize.width * 0.5, _player1-
>radius() * 2));
this->addChild(_player1);


_player2 = GameSprite::gameSpriteWithFile("mallet.png");
_player2->setPosition(ccp(_screenSize.width * 0.5, _screenSize.
height - _player1->radius() * 2));
this->addChild(_player2);
_ball = GameSprite::gameSpriteWithFile("puck.png");
_ball->setPosition(ccp(_screenSize.width * 0.5, _screenSize.height
* 0.5 - 2 * _ball->radius()));
this->addChild(_ball);
```

5. We create a CCArray method to store the player objects and we retain this array to keep a reference to it throughout the game:

```
_players = CCArray::create(_player1, _player2, NULL);
_players->retain();
```

6. We create labels with the CCLabelTTF class, passing as parameters: the initial string value (0), the font name, and size (once again the font size will be automatically scaled in the high definition version). We then position and rotate the labels:

```
_player1ScoreLabel = CCLabelTTF::create("0", "Arial", 60);
_player1ScoreLabel->setPosition(ccp(_screenSize.width - 60, _
screenSize.height * 0.5 - 80));
_player1ScoreLabel->setRotation(90);
this->addChild(_player1ScoreLabel);
```

```
_player2ScoreLabel = CCLabelTTF::create("0", "Arial", 60);
_player2ScoreLabel->setPosition(ccp(_screenSize.width - 60, _
screenSize.height * 0.5 + 80));
_player2ScoreLabel->setRotation(90);
this->addChild(_player2ScoreLabel);
```

Label objects (CCLabelTTF) can use any of the fonts supported by the target system; these change from system to system, however. But there is an option of loading your own TTF files.

7. Finish off by declaring that your CCLayer wishes to listen for touches and by scheduling the game's main loop as follows:

```
//listen for touches
this->setTouchEnabled(true);
//create main loop
this->schedule(schedule_selector(GameLayer::update));
return true;
```

What just happened?

You created the game screen for Air Hockey, with your own sprites and labels. Don't forget to release the _players array we retained. Do it in the destructor as follows:

```
GameLayer::~GameLayer() {
    CC_SAFE_RELEASE(_players);
}
```

The CC_SAFE_RELEASE macro will check to see if _players is not NULL before releasing it.

The game screen, once all elements are added, should look like this:

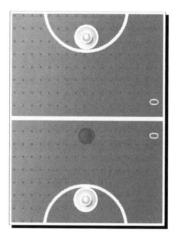

And now we're ready to handle the players' screen touches.

Time for action — handling multi-touches

There are three methods we need to implement in this game to handle touches. Each method receives as one of its parameters a CCSet object containing the touches (and CCSet means we are about to use iterators).

1. First we add our `ccTouchesBegan` method:

```
void GameLayer::ccTouchesBegan(CCSet* pTouches, CCEvent* event) {
    CCSetIterator i;
    CCTouch* touch;
    CCPoint tap;
    GameSprite * player;

    for( i = pTouches->begin(); i != pTouches->end(); i++) {
        touch = (CCTouch*) (*i);
        if(touch) {
            tap = touch->getLocation();
            for (int p = 0; p < 2; p++) {
                player = (GameSprite *) _players-
                >objectAtIndex(p);
                if (player->boundingBox().containsPoint(tap)) {
                player->setTouch(touch);
                }
            }
        }
    }
}
```

Each `GameSprite`, if you recall, has a `_touch` property.

So we iterate through the touches, grab their location on screen, loop through the players in the array, and determine if the touch lands on one of the players. If so, we store the touch inside the player's `_touch` property (from the `GameSprite` class).

A similar process is repeated for `ccTouchesMoved` and `ccTouchesEnded`, so you may copy and paste the code and just replace what goes on inside the `_players` array for loop.

2. In `ccTouchesMoved`, when we loop through the players we do this:

```
for (int p = 0; p < _players->count(); p++) {
    player = (GameSprite *) _players->objectAtIndex(p);

    if (player->getTouch() != NULL && player->getTouch() ==
    touch) {
```

```
CCPoint nextPosition = tap;
//keep player inside screen
if (nextPosition.x < player->radius())
    nextPosition.x = player->radius();
    if (nextPosition.x > _screenSize.width - player-
    >radius())
        nextPosition.x = _screenSize.width - player-
        >radius();


    if (nextPosition.y < player->radius())
       nextPosition.y  = player->radius();


    if (nextPosition.y > _screenSize.height - player-
    >radius())
  nextPosition.y = _screenSize.height - player->radius();



     //keep player inside its court
    if (player->getPositionY() < _screenSize.height *
    0.5f)
    {
      if (nextPosition.y >
      _screenSize.height * 0.5 - player->radius())
      {
          nextPosition.y =
          _screenSize.height * 0.5 - player-
          >radius();
      }

      } else {
      if (nextPosition.y <
      _screenSize.height * 0.5 + player->radius())
      {
          nextPosition.y =
          _screenSize.height * 0.5 + player-
          >radius();
      }
      }

    player->setNextPosition(nextPosition);
    player->setVector(ccp(tap.x - player->getPositionX(),
    tap.y - player->getPositionY()));
  }
}
```

We check to see if the `_touch` property stored inside the player is the same being moved now. If so, we update the player's position with the touch's current position, but we check to see if the new position is valid: a player cannot move outside the screen and cannot enter their opponent's court. We also update the player's vector of movement, which we'll need when we collide the player with the puck. The vector is based on the player's displacement.

3. In `ccTouchesEnded` we add this:

```
for (int p = 0; p < _players->count(); p++) {
    player = (GameSprite *) _players->objectAtIndex(p);

    if (player->getTouch() != NULL && player->getTouch() ==
    touch) {
        player->setTouch(NULL);
        player->setVector(ccp(0,0));););
    }
}
```

We clear the `_touch` stored inside the player if this touch is the one just ending. The player also stops moving, so its vector is set to 0. Notice that we don't need the location of the touch anymore, so in `ccTouchesEnded` you may skip that bit of logic.

What just happened?

When you implement logic for multi-touch this is pretty much what you will have to do: store the individual touches inside either an array or individual sprites, so you can keep tracking these touches.

The other option is to make your nodes implement a protocol called `CCTargetedTouchDelegate`. But this may result in the implementation of up to eight methods.

You may go to the test code in `samples/TestCpp/Classes/TouchesTest` and review the code used in the `Paddle.h` and `Paddle.cpp` files for an example of `CCTargetedTouchDelegate` in action.

Now, for the heart and soul of the game: the main loop.

Time for action – adding our main loop

This is the heart of our game - the `update` method:

1. We update the puck's velocity, with a little friction applied to its vector (`0.98f`). We store what its next position will be at the end of the iteration, if no collision occurred:

```
void GameLayer::update (float dt) {

    CCPoint ballNextPosition = _ball->getNextPosition();
    CCPoint ballVector = _ball->getVector();
    ballVector = ccpMult(ballVector, 0.98f);

    ballNextPosition.x += ballVector.x;
    ballNextPosition.y += ballVector.y;
```

2. Next comes collision. We check collision between each player sprite and the ball:

```
GameSprite * player;
CCPoint playerNextPosition;
CCPoint playerVector;

float squared_radii = pow(_player1->radius() + _ball->radius(),
2);
for (int p = 0; p < _players->count(); p++) {

    player = (GameSprite *) _players->objectAtIndex(p);
    playerNextPosition = player->getNextPosition();
    playerVector = player->getVector();

    float diffx = ballNextPosition.x - player->getPositionX();
    float diffy = ballNextPosition.y - player->getPositionY();

    float distance1 = pow(diffx, 2) + pow(diffy, 2);
    float distance2 = pow(_ball->getPositionX() -
    playerNextPosition.x, 2) +
        pow(_ball->getPositionY() -
    playerNextPosition.y, 2);
```

Collision is checked through the distance between ball and players. Two conditions will flag a collision, as illustrated in the following image.

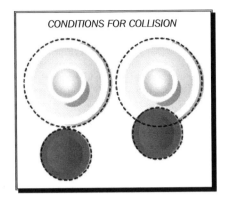

CONDITIONS FOR COLLISION

3. If the distance between ball and player is less than or equal to the sum of the radii of both sprites we have a collision:

```
if (distance1 <= squared_radii ||
    distance2 <= squared_radii)  {
```

4. We use the squared radii values so we don't need to use costly square root calculations to get the values for distance. So all values in the previous conditional statement are squared, including the distances.

5. These conditions are checked both with the player's current position and its next position, so there is less risk of the ball moving "through" the player sprite between iterations.

6. If there is a collision, we grab the magnitudes of both the ball's vector and the player's vector, and calculate the force with which the ball will be pushed away. We update the ball's next position in that case, and play a nice sound effect through the `SimpleAudioEngine` singleton:

```
float mag_ball = pow(ballVector.x, 2) + pow(ballVector.y,
2);
float mag_player = pow(playerVector.x, 2) + pow
(playerVector.y, 2);
float force = sqrt(mag_ball + mag_player);
float angle = atan2(diffy, diffx);

    ballVector.x = force * cos(angle);
    ballVector.y = (force * sin(angle));

    ballNextPosition.x = playerNextPosition.x + (player-
    >radius() + _ball->radius() + force) * cos(angle);
    ballNextPosition.y = playerNextPosition.y + (player-
    >radius() + _ball->radius() + force) * sin(angle);
```

```
        SimpleAudioEngine::sharedEngine()-
        >playEffect("hit.wav");
    }
}
```

7. Next, check for collision between ball and screen sides. If found, we move the ball
back into the court and play our sound effect here as well:

```
if (ballNextPosition.x < _ball->radius()) {
    ballNextPosition.x = _ball->radius();
    ballVector.x *= -0.8f;
    SimpleAudioEngine::sharedEngine()->playEffect("hit.wav");
}
```

```
if (ballNextPosition.x > _screenSize.width - _ball->radius()) {
    ballNextPosition.x = _screenSize.width - _ball->radius();
    ballVector.x *= -0.8f;
    SimpleAudioEngine::sharedEngine()->playEffect("hit.wav");
}
```

8. At the top and bottom sides of the court we check to see if the ball has not moved
through one of the goals through our previously defined GOAL_WIDTH property,
as follows:

```
if (ballNextPosition.y > _screenSize.height - _ball->radius()) {
    if (_ball->getPosition().x < _screenSize.width * 0.5f -
    GOAL_WIDTH * 0.5f || _ball->getPosition().x >
    _screenSize.width * 0.5f + GOAL_WIDTH * 0.5f) {
        ballNextPosition.y = _screenSize.height - _ball-
        >radius();
        ballVector.y *= -0.8f;
        SimpleAudioEngine::sharedEngine()-
        >playEffect("hit.wav");
    }
}
```

```
if (ballNextPosition.y < _ball->radius() ) {
    if (_ball->getPosition().x < _screenSize.width * 0.5f -
    GOAL_WIDTH * 0.5f || _ball->getPosition().x >
    _screenSize.width * 0.5f + GOAL_WIDTH * 0.5f) {
        ballNextPosition.y = _ball->radius();
        ballVector.y *= -0.8f;
        SimpleAudioEngine::sharedEngine()-
        >playEffect("hit.wav");
    }
}
```

9. We finally update the ball information, and if the ball has passed through the goal posts (drum roll):

```
_ball->setVector(ballVector);
_ball->setNextPosition(ballNextPosition);

//check for goals!
if (ballNextPosition.y  < -_ball->radius() * 2) {
   this->playerScore(2);
}

if (ballNextPosition.y > _screenSize.height + _ball->radius() * 2)
{
    this->playerScore(1);
}
```

10. We call our helper method to score a point, and we finish the update with the placement of all the elements, now that we know where the nextPosition is for each one of the elements in the game:

```
_player1->setPosition(_player1->getNextPosition());
_player2->setPosition(_player2->getNextPosition());
_ball->setPosition(_ball->getNextPosition());
```

What just happened?

We have just built the game's main loop. Whenever your gameplay depends on precise collision detection you will undoubtedly apply a similar logic of: position now, position next, collision checks, and adjustments to position next, if any collision has occurred.

And we finish the game with our helper method.

All that's left to do now is to update the scores.

Time for action – updating scores

Time to type the last method in the game:

1. We start by playing a nice effect for a goal and stopping our ball:

```
void GameLayer::playerScore (int player) {

    SimpleAudioEngine::sharedEngine()->playEffect("score.wav");

    _ball->setVector(ccp(0,0));
```

2. Then we update the score for the scoring player, updating the score label in the process. And the ball moves to the court of the player against whom a point was just scored:

```
char score_buffer[10];
if (player == 1) {
    _player1Score++;
    sprintf(score_buffer,"%i", _player1Score);
    _player1ScoreLabel->setString(score_buffer);
    _ball->setNextPosition(ccp(_screenSize.width * 0.5,
    _screenSize.height * 0.5 + 2 * _ball->radius()));

    } else {
    _player2Score++;
    sprintf(score_buffer,"%i", _player2Score);
    _player2ScoreLabel->setString(score_buffer);
    _ball->setNextPosition(ccp(_screenSize.width * 0.5,
    _screenSize.height * 0.5 - 2 * _ball->radius()));
    }
```

The players are moved to their original position and their _touch properties are cleared:

```
    _player1->setPosition(ccp(_screenSize.width * 0.5,
    _player1->radius() * 2));
    _player2->setPosition(ccp(_screenSize.width * 0.5,
    _screenSize.height - _player1->radius() * 2));
    _player1->setTouch(NULL);
    _player2->setTouch(NULL);
}
```

3. Non-C++ programmers should pay attention to the way strings are formed from integers:

```
char score_buffer[10];
sprintf(score_buffer,"%i", _player1Score);
```

4. Although you could also use CCObject-derived CCString:

```
CCString * score = CCString::createWithFormat("%i", _
player1Score);
_player1ScoreLabel->setString(score->getCString());
```

What just happened?

Well, guess what? You just finished your first game in Cocos2d-x. We charged forward at a brisk pace, for our first game, but we managed to touch on almost every area of game development with Cocos2d-x in the process.

If you click **Run** now you should be able to play the game. In the source code for this chapter you should also find the complete version of the game if you run into any problems.

Have a go hero

In the RESOURCES.zip file you downloaded there is a logo.png image. As an exercise, place this logo in the middle of the screen at the beginning of the game and don't update the game while the logo is visible (CCSprite ->isVisible() property). Then when the user touches the screen if the logo is visible, hide it (CCSprite ->setVisible(false)) and return from the function.

Summary

You have now seen how to add sprites and labels, how to add support for two screen resolutions as well as support for multi-touch. There are quite a few ways to create CCSprites other than by passing it an image file name, and I'll show examples of these in the games to come.

CCLabelTTF won't be used as much from now on. Generally they are good for large chunks of text and text that is not updated too frequently; we'll use bitmap fonts from now on.

So, let's move on to the next game and animations. I promise I won't make you type as much. You should get your friend to do it for you.

4

Fun with Sprites – Sky Defense

Time to build our second game! This time you will become acquainted with the power of actions in Cocos2d-x. I'll show you how an entire game can be built just by running the various action commands contained in Cocos2d-x, to make your sprites move, rotate, scale, fade, blink, and so on. And you can also use actions to animate your sprites by using multiple images, as in a movie. So let's get started.

In this chapter you will learn:

- How to optimize development of your game by using sprite sheets
- How to use bitmap fonts in your game
- How easy it is to implement and run CCActions
- How to scale, rotate, swing, move, and fade out a sprite
- How to load multiple .png files and use them to animate a sprite
- How to create a universal game with Cocos2d-x

The game – Sky Defense

Meet our stressed out city of... your name of choice here. It's a beautiful day, when suddenly the sky begins to fall. There are meteors rushing towards the city and it is your job to keep it safe.

The player in this game can tap the screen to start growing a bomb. When the bomb is big enough to be activated, the player taps the screen again to detonate it. Any nearby meteor will explode into a million pieces. The bigger the bomb, the bigger the detonation and the more meteors can be taken out by it. But the bigger the bomb, the longer it takes to grow it.

But it's not just bad news coming down. There are also health packs dropping from the sky and if you allow them to reach the ground, you'll recover some of your energy.

The game settings

This is a universal game. It is designed for the iPad retina screen and it will be scaled down to fit other screens. The game will be played in landscape mode, and it will not need to support multi-touch.

The start project

Go ahead and download the file `7341_04_START_PROJECT.zip` from this book's support page (`www.packtpub.com/support`). When you uncompress the file, you will find the basic project already set up and ready for you to work on.

The steps involved in creating this project are similar to the ones I showed you in our previous game. Only this time, the **Device Family** is set to **Universal**. And in `RootViewController.mm`, the supported interface orientation is set to **Landscape**.

The game we are going to build requires only one class, `GameLayer.cpp`, and you will find that the interface for this class already contains all of the information it needs.

Also, some of the more trivial or old-news logic is already in place in the implementation file as well. But I'll go over this as we work on the game.

Adding screen support for a universal app

In the previous game we targeted iPad-size screens only. Now things get a bit more complicated as we add support for smaller screens in our universal game.

So open `AppDelegate.cpp`. Inside the `applicationDidFinishLaunching` method we now have the following code:

```
CCSize screenSize = pEGLView->getFrameSize();
CCSize designSize = CCSize(2048, 1536);

CCEGLView::sharedOpenGLView()->setDesignResolutionSize
    (designSize.width, designSize.height, kResolutionExactFit);

if (screenSize.height > 768) {
```

```
    CCFileUtils::sharedFileUtils()->setResourceDirectory("ipadhd");
} else if (screenSize.height > 320) {
    CCFileUtils::sharedFileUtils()->setResourceDirectory("ipad");
} else {
    CCFileUtils::sharedFileUtils()->setResourceDirectory("iphone");
}
pDirector->setContentScaleFactor
    (screenSize.height/designSize.height);
```

Once again we tell our CCEGLView object (our OpenGL view) that we have designed the game for a certain screen size (the iPad retina screen) and once again we want our game screen to resize to match the screen on the device (kResolutionExactFit).

Then we determine where to load our images from, based on the device's screen size. We have art for iPad retina, then for a regular iPad which is shared by iPhone retina, and finally for the regular iPhone.

We end by setting the scale factor based on the designed target.

Adding background music

Still inside AppDelegate.cpp, we load the sound files that we'll use in the game, including a background.mp3 (courtesy of *Kevin MacLeod* from incompetech.com), which we load through the command:

```
SimpleAudioEngine::sharedEngine()->preloadBackgroundMusic(file);
```

We end by setting the effects volume down a tad:

```
//lower playback volume for effects
SimpleAudioEngine::sharedEngine()->setEffectsVolume(0.4f);
```

For background music volume, you must use setBackgroundMusicVolume. If you create some sort of volume control in your game, these are the calls you would make to adjust the volume based on the user's preference.

Initializing the game

Now back to GameLayer.cpp. If you take a look inside our init method, you will see that the game initializes by calling three methods: createGameScreen, createPools, and createActions.

We'll create all our screen elements inside the first method, then create object pools so we don't instantiate any sprite inside the main loop; and we'll create all of the main actions used in our game inside the createActions method.

There is a `CCArray` called `_fallingObjects` also created here, and we start playing the background music, with the loop flag set to `true`:

```
SimpleAudioEngine::sharedEngine()-
    >playBackgroundMusic("background.mp3", true);
```

We once again store the screen size for future reference, and we'll use a `_running` Boolean for game states.

But if you run the game now, you will only see the background image:

Using sprite sheets in Cocos2d-x

A sprite sheet is a way to group multiple images together into one image file. In order to texture a sprite with one of these images you must have the information of where in the sprite sheet that particular image is found (its rectangle).

Sprite sheets are often organized into two files: the image file and a data file that describes where in the image you can find the individual textures.

I used `TexturePacker` to create these files for the game. You can find them inside the ipad, ipadhd, and iphone folders inside `Resources`. There is a `sprite_sheet.png` for the image and a `sprite_sheet.plist` that describes the individual frames inside the image.

This is what the `sprite_sheet.png` file looks like:

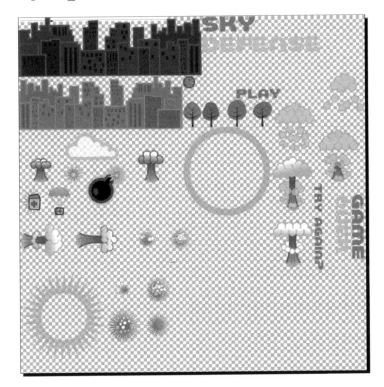

Batch drawing sprites

In Cocos2d-x, sprite sheets can be used in conjunction with a specialized CCNode called
CCSpriteBatchNode. This node may be used whenever you wish to use multiple sprites
that share the same source image inside the same node. So you could have multiple
instances of a CCSprite that uses a `bullet.png` texture, for instance. And if the source
image is a sprite sheet then you can have multiple instances of sprites displaying as many
different textures as you can pack inside your sprite sheet.

With CCSpriteBatchNode, you can substantially reduce the number of calls during the
rendering stage of your game, which will help when targeting less powerful systems, though
not noticeably in the Apple device family.

Let me show you how to create a CCSpriteBatchNode.

Time for action – creating a CCSpriteBatchNode

Let's begin implementing the `createGameScreen` method in `GameLayer.cpp`. Just below the lines that add the `bg` sprite, we instantiate our batch node:

```
void GameLayer::createGameScreen() {

  //add bg
  CCSprite * bg = CCSprite::create("bg.png");
  ...


  CCSpriteFrameCache::sharedSpriteFrameCache()->
  addSpriteFramesWithFile("sprite_sheet.plist");

  _gameBatchNode = CCSpriteBatchNode::create("sprite_sheet.png");
  this->addChild(_gameBatchNode);
```

In order to create the batch node from a sprite sheet, we first load all of the frame information described by the `sprite_sheet.plist` file into `CCSpriteFrameCache`. And then we create the batch node with the `sprite_sheet.png` file, which is the source texture shared by all sprites added to this batch node. (The background image is not part of the sprite sheet, so it's added separately, before we add `_gameBatchNode` to `GameLayer`.)

Perform the given steps to add sprites to a CCSpriteBatchNode:

1. Now we can start putting things inside `_gameBatchNode`. First the city:

```
CCSprite * sprite;
for (int i = 0; i < 2; i++) {
  sprite = CCSprite::createWithSpriteFrameName
  ("city_dark.png");
  sprite->setPosition(ccp(
    _screenSize.width * (0.25f + i * 0.5f),
  sprite->boundingBox().size.height * 0.5f));
  _gameBatchNode->addChild(sprite, kForeground);

  sprite = CCSprite::createWithSpriteFrameName
  ("city_light.png");
  sprite->setPosition(ccp(
    _screenSize.width * (0.25f + i * 0.5f),
  sprite->boundingBox().size.height * 0.9f));
  _gameBatchNode->addChild(sprite, kBackground);
}
```

2. Then we add the trees:

```
//add trees
for (int i = 0; i < 3; i++) {
  sprite = CCSprite::createWithSpriteFrameName("trees.png");
  sprite->setPosition(ccp(
    _screenSize.width * (0.2f + i * 0.3f),
  sprite->boundingBox().size.height * 0.5f));
  _gameBatchNode->addChild(sprite, kForeground);


}
```

Notice that here we create CCSprites by passing it a sprite frame name. The IDs for these frame names were loaded into CCSpriteFrameCache through our sprite_sheet.plist file.

3. The screen so far is made up of two instances of city_dark.png tiling at the bottom of the screen, and two instances of city_light.png that are also tiling. One needs to appear on top of the other, and for that we use the enumerated values declared in GameLayer.h:

```
enum {
  kBackground,
  kMiddleground,
  kForeground
};
```

4. We use the addChild(CCNode, zOrder) method to layer our sprites on top of each other, using different values for their z order.

So for example, when we later add three sprites showing the trees.png sprite frame, we add them on top of all previous sprites by using the highest value for z that we find in the enumerated list kForeground.

 Why go to the trouble of tiling the images and not using one large image instead, or combining some of them with the background image? Because I wanted to include the greatest number of images possible inside the one sprite sheet, and have that sprite sheet be as small as possible, to illustrate all the clever ways in which you can use and optimize sprite sheets, even though this is not necessary in this particular game.

What just happened?

We have begun to create the initial screen for our game. We are using a
CCSpriteBatchNode to contain all of the sprites that use images from our sprite sheet.
So CCSpriteBatchNode behaves as any node does: as a container. And we can layer
individual CCSprites inside the batch node by manipulating their z order.

Bitmap fonts in Cocos2d-x

The Cocos2d-x CCLabelBMFont class uses bitmap images for the characters, unlike
CCLabelTTF which uses true type font files.

The bitmap image we are using here was created with the program **GlyphDesigner**, and in
essence it works just as a sprite sheet does. As a matter of fact, CCLabelBMFont extends
CCSpriteBatchNode, so it behaves just like a batch node.

You have images for all of the individual characters that you'll need packed inside a *PNG* file
(font.png), and then a data file (font.fnt) describing where each character is.

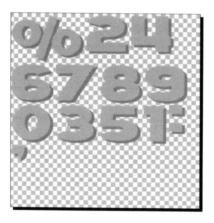

The difference between CCLabelBMFont and a regular CCSpriteBatchNode is that the
data file also feeds the CCLabelBMFont object information on how to "write" with this font.
In other words, how to space out the characters and lines correctly.

The CCLabelBMFont objects that we are using in the game are instantiated with their initial
string value, the name of the data file, and the total width of the label object.

```
_scoreDisplay = CCLabelBMFont::create
    ("0", "font.fnt", _screenSize.width * 0.3f);
```

The value for the label is changed through the `setString` method.

```
_scoreDisplay->setString("My new Label");
```

 Just as with every other image in the game, we also have different versions of `font.fnt` and `font.png` in our resource folders, one for each screen definition. `CCFileUtils` once again will do the heavy lifting of finding the correct file for the correct screen.

So now let's create the labels for our game.

Time for action – creating bitmap font labels

Creating a bitmap font is somewhat similar to creating a batch node.

1. Continuing with our `createGameScreen` method, add the following lines to the score label:

```
_scoreDisplay = CCLabelBMFont::create
    ("0", "font.fnt", _screenSize.width * 0.3f);
_scoreDisplay->setAnchorPoint(ccp(1,0.5));
_scoreDisplay->setPosition(ccp
    (_screenSize.width * 0.8f, _screenSize.height * 0.94f));
this->addChild(_scoreDisplay);
```

And then add a label to display the energy level:

```
_energyDisplay = CCLabelBMFont::create
    ("100%", "font.fnt", _screenSize.width * 0.1f,
kCCTextAlignmentRight);
_energyDisplay->setPosition(ccp
    (_screenSize.width * 0.3f, _screenSize.height * 0.94f));
this->addChild(_energyDisplay);
```

2. Add the following line for an icon that appears next to the `_energyDisplay` label:

```
CCSprite * icon = CCSprite::createWithSpriteFrameName
    ("health_icon.png");
icon->setPosition( ccp(_screenSize.
    width * 0.15f, _screenSize.height * 0.94f) );
_gameBatchNode->addChild(icon, kBackground);
```

What just happened?

We just created our first bitmap font object in Cocos2d-x.

 By using setAnchorPoint () in our label objects, we can make sure that the label is aligned correctly on screen when updated. So for instance, with _scoreDisplay, we setAnchorPoint x to 1—the right-hand side of the label—so when the label grows it remains fixed on its right side, and grows towards the left of the screen.

Now let's finish creating our game's sprites.

Time for action – adding the final screen sprites

The last sprites that we need to create are the clouds, the bomb and shockwave, and our game state messages.

1. Back to the createGameScreen method, add the clouds to the screen:

```
CCSprite * cloud;
_clouds = CCArray::createWithCapacity(4);
_clouds->retain();
float cloud_y;

for (int i = 0; i < 4; i++) {
  cloud_y = i % 2 == 0 ? _screenSize.height * 0.4f :
  _screenSize.height * 0.5f;
  cloud = CCSprite::createWithSpriteFrameName("cloud.png");
  cloud->setPosition(ccp (_screenSize.width * 0.1f + i *
  _screenSize.width * 0.3f,  cloud_y));
  _gameBatchNode->addChild(cloud, kBackground);
  _clouds->addObject(cloud);
}
```

2. Create the _bomb sprite that the players will "grow" when tapping the screen:

```
_bomb = CCSprite::createWithSpriteFrameName("bomb.png");
_bomb->getTexture()->generateMipmap();
_bomb->setVisible(false);

CCSize size = _bomb->boundingBox().size;

//add sparkle inside bomb sprite
CCSprite * sparkle = CCSprite::createWithSpriteFrameName("sparkle.
png");
```

```
sparkle->setPosition(ccp(size.width * 0.72f, size.height *
    0.72f));
_bomb->addChild(sparkle, kMiddleground, kSpriteSparkle);

//add halo inside bomb sprite
CCSprite * halo = CCSprite::createWithSpriteFrameName
    ("halo.png");
halo->setPosition(ccp(size.width * 0.4f, size.height *
    0.4f));
_bomb->addChild(halo, kMiddleground, kSpriteHalo);
_gameBatchNode->addChild(_bomb, kForeground);
```

3. Then create the _shockwave sprite that appears after the _bomb goes off:

```
_shockWave = CCSprite::createWithSpriteFrameName
    ("shockwave.png");
_shockWave->getTexture()->generateMipmap();
_shockWave->setVisible(false);
_gameBatchNode->addChild(_shockWave);
```

4. Finally, add the two messages that appear on the screen, one for our intro state, and one for our game over state:

```
_introMessage = CCSprite::createWithSpriteFrameName
    ("logo.png");
_introMessage->setPosition(ccp
    (_screenSize.width * 0.5f, _screenSize.height * 0.6f));
_introMessage->setVisible(true);
this->addChild(_introMessage, kForeground);

_gameOverMessage = CCSprite::createWithSpriteFrameName
    ("gameover.png");
_gameOverMessage->setPosition(ccp
    (_screenSize.width * 0.5f, _screenSize.height * 0.65f));
_gameOverMessage->setVisible(false);
this->addChild(_gameOverMessage, kForeground);
```

What just happened?

There is a lot of new information regarding sprites in the previous code, so let's go over it carefully:

- We started by adding the clouds. We put the sprites inside a CCArray so we can move the clouds later. Notice they are also part of our batch node.

- Next comes the bomb sprite and our first new call:

  ```
  _bomb->getTexture()->generateMipmap();
  ```

- With this, we are telling the framework to create antialiased copies of this texture in diminishing sizes (mipmaps), since we are going to scale it down later. This is optional of course, as sprites can be resized without first generating mipmaps, but if you notice a loss of quality in the scaled sprites, you can fix it by creating mipmaps for their texture.

> The texture must have size values in so-called POT (power of two: 2, 4, 8, 16, 32, 64, 128, 256, 512, 1024, 2048, and so on.) Textures in OpenGL must always be sized this way; when they are not, Cocos2d-x will do one of two things: it will resize the texture in memory, adding transparent pixels until the image reaches a POT size, or stop the execution on an `Assert`. With textures used for mipmaps the framework will stop execution for non-POT textures.

- I add the `sparkle` and the `halo` sprites as children to the `_bomb` sprite. This will use the container characteristic of `CCNodes` to our advantage. When I grow the bomb, all of its children will grow with it.

- Notice, too, that I use a third parameter to `addChild` for `halo` and `sparkle`:

```
bomb->addChild(halo, kMiddleground, kSpriteHalo);
```

- This third parameter is an integer tag, from yet another enumerated list declared in `GameLayer.h`. I can use this tag to retrieve a particular child from a sprite, like this:

```
CCSprite * halo = (CCSprite *)
    bomb->getChildByTag(kSpriteHalo);
```

We now have our game screen in place:

Next come object pools.

Time for action – creating our object pools

The pools are just arrays of objects. Here are the steps to create them:

1. Inside the `createPools` method, we first create a pool for meteors:

```
void GameLayer::createPools() {
  CCSprite * sprite;
  int i;

  _meteorPool = CCArray::createWithCapacity(50);
  _meteorPool->retain();
  _meteorPoolIndex = 0;
  for (i = 0; i < 50; i++) {
    sprite = CCSprite::createWithSpriteFrameName
    ("meteor.png");
    sprite->setVisible(false);
    _gameBatchNode->addChild
    (sprite, kMiddleground, kSpriteMeteor);
    _meteorPool->addObject(sprite);
  }
```

2. Then we create an object pool for health packs:

```
  _healthPool = CCArray::createWithCapacity(20);
  _healthPool->retain();
  _healthPoolIndex = 0;
  for (i = 0; i < 20; i++) {
    sprite = CCSprite::createWithSpriteFrameName
    ("health.png");
    sprite->setVisible(false);
    sprite->setAnchorPoint(ccp(0.5f, 0.8f));
    _gameBatchNode->addChild
    (sprite, kMiddleground, kSpriteHealth);
    _healthPool->addObject(sprite);
  }
}
```

3. We'll use the corresponding pool index to retrieve objects from the arrays as the game progresses.

What just happened?

We now have an array of invisible meteor sprites and an array of invisible health sprites. We'll use their respective pool indices to retrieve these from the array as needed, as you'll see in a moment. But first we need to take care of actions and animations.

By using object pools we reduce the number of instantiations during the main loop, and it allows us to never destroy anything that can be reused. But if you need to remove a child from a node use either ->removeChild, or ->removeChildByTag if a tag is present.

CCActions in a nutshell

If you remember, a CCNode will store information about the position, scale, rotation, visibility, and opacity of a node. And in Cocos2d-x, there is a CCAction class to change each one of these values over time, in effect animating these transformations.

Actions are usually created with a static method create. The majority of these actions are time-based, so usually the first parameter that you need to pass to an action is the time length for the action. So for instance:

```
CCFadeOut *fadeout = CCFadeOut::create(1.0f);
```

This creates a fade-out action that will take one second to complete. You may run it on a sprite, or node, like this:

```
mySprite->runAction(fadeout);
```

Cocos2d-x has an incredibly flexible system that allows us to create any combination of actions and transformations to achieve any effect we desire.

You may, for instance, choose to create an action sequence (CCSequence) that contains more than one action; or you can apply easing effects (CCEaseIn, CCEaseOut, and so on) to your actions. You can choose to repeat an action a certain number of times (CCRepeat) or forever (CCRepeatForever); and you may add callbacks to functions that you want to be called once an action is completed (usually inside a CCSequence).

Time for action – creating actions with Cocos2d-x

Creating actions with Cocos2d-x is a very simple process.

1. Inside our createActions method we will instantiate the actions that we can use repeatedly in our game. Let's create our first actions:

```
void GameLayer::createActions() {

    //swing action for health drops
    CCFiniteTimeAction* easeSwing =
        CCSequence::create(
            CCEaseInOut::create(CCRotateTo::create(1.2f, -10), 2),
```

```
      CCEaseInOut::create(CCRotateTo::create(1.2f, 10), 2),
NULL);
_swingHealth = CCRepeatForever::create
( (CCActionInterval*) easeSwing );
_swingHealth->retain();
```

2. Actions can be combined in many different forms. Here, the retained `_swingHealth` action is a `CCRepeatForever` of a `CCSequence` that will rotate the health sprite first one way, then the other, with a `CCEaseInOut` wrapping the `CCRotateTo` action. `CCRotateTo` takes 1.2 seconds to rotate the sprite first to -10 degrees and then to 10. And the easing has a value of 2, which I suggest you experiment with to get a sense of what it means visually. Next we add three more actions:

```
//action sequence for shockwave: fade out, callback when
//done
_shockwaveSequence =
  CCSequence::create(
    CCFadeOut::create(1.0f),
    CCCallFunc::create
    (this, callfunc_selector(GameLayer::shockwaveDone)),
  NULL);
_shockwaveSequence->retain();

//action to grow bomb
_growBomb = CCScaleTo::create(6.0f, 1.0);
_growBomb->retain();

//action to rotate sprites
CCActionInterval*  rotate = CCRotateBy::create(0.5f ,  -90);
_rotateSprite = CCRepeatForever::create( rotate );
_rotateSprite->retain();
```

First, another `CCSequence`. This will fade out the sprite and call the function `shockwaveDone`, which is already implemented in the class, and which turns the `_shockwave` sprite invisible when called.

The last one is a `CCRepeatForever` of a `CCRotateBy` action. In half a second the sprite running this action will rotate -90 degrees, then again, and again, and again.

What just happened?

You just got your first glimpse at creating actions in Cocos2d-x and at how the framework allows for all sorts of combinations to accomplish any effect.

It may be hard at first to read through a CCSequence and understand what's happening, but the logic is easy to follow once you break it down into its individual parts.

But we are not done with the createActions method yet. Next comes sprite animations.

Animating a sprite in Cocos2d-x

The key thing to remember is that an animation is just another type of CCAction—one that changes the texture used by a CCSprite over a period of time.

In order to create an animation action you need to first create a CCAnimation object. This object will store all of the information regarding the different sprite frames that you wish to use in the animation, the length of the animation in seconds, and whether it loops or not.

With this CCAnimation object you then create a CCAnimate action. Let's take a look.

Time for action – creating animations

Animations are a specialized type of action that require a few extra steps.

1. Inside the same method, createActions, add the lines for the two animations that we have in the game. First, add the animation that shows an explosion when a meteor reaches the city. We begin by loading the frames into a CCAnimation object:

```
CCAnimation* animation;
CCSpriteFrame * frame;

//create CCAnimation object
animation = CCAnimation::create();
CCString * name;
for(int i = 1; i <= 10; i++) {
    name = CCString::createWithFormat("boom%i.png", i);
    frame = CCSpriteFrameCache::sharedSpriteFrameCache()-
    >spriteFrameByName(name->getCString());
    animation->addSpriteFrame(frame);
}
```

2. Then we use the animation object inside a CCAnimate action:

```
animation->setDelayPerUnit(1 / 10.0f);
animation->setRestoreOriginalFrame(true);
_groundHit =
    CCSequence::create(
        CCMoveBy::create(0, ccp(0,_screenSize.height * 0.12f)),
        CCAnimate::create(animation),
```

```
    CCCallFuncN::create
      (this, callfuncN_selector(GameLayer::animationDone)),
   NULL);
_groundHit->retain();
```

3. The same steps are repeated to create the other explosion animation, which is used when the player hits a meteor or a health pack.

```
animation = CCAnimation::create();
for(int i = 1; i <= 7; i++) {
  name = CCString::createWithFormat
  ("explosion_small%i.png", i);
frame = CCSpriteFrameCache::sharedSpriteFrameCache()
  ->spriteFrameByName(name->getCString());
  animation->addSpriteFrame(frame);
}

animation->setDelayPerUnit(0.5 / 7.0f);
animation->setRestoreOriginalFrame(true);
_explosion = CCSequence::create(
  CCAnimate::create(animation),
  CCCallFuncN::create(this, callfuncN_selector
  (GameLayer::animationDone)),
  NULL);
_explosion->retain();
```

What just happened?

We created two instances of a very special kind of action in Cocos2d-x: `CCAnimate`. Here is what we did:

- First we created a `CCAnimation` object. This object holds the references to all the textures used in the animation. The frames were named in such a way that they can easily be concatenated inside a loop (boom1, boom2, boom3, and so on) There are ten frames for the first animation and seven for the second.

- The textures (or frames) are `CCSpriteFrame` objects that we grab from the `CCSpriteFrameCache`, which, as you remember, contains all of the information from the `sprite_sheet.plist` data file. So the frames are in our sprite sheet.

- Then, when all frames are in place, we determine the delay of each frame by dividing the total amount of seconds for which we want the animation to last by the total number of frames.

- The `setRestoreOriginalFrame` method is important here. If we set `setRestoreOriginalFrame` to `true`, then the sprite will revert to its original appearance once the animation is over. For example, if I have an explosion animation which will run on a meteor sprite; by the end of the explosion animation, the sprite will revert to displaying the meteor texture.

- Then comes the actual action. `CCAnimate` receives the `CCAnimation` object as its parameter. (In the first animation we shift the position of the sprite just before the explosion appears, so there is an extra `CCMoveBy`.)

- In both instances I make a call to an `animationDone` callback already implemented in the class. This makes the calling sprite invisible:

```
void GameLayer::animationDone (CCNode* pSender) {
  pSender->setVisible(false);
}
```

We could have used the same method for both callbacks (`animationDone` and `shockwaveDone`) as they accomplish the same thing. But I wanted to show you a callback that receives as an argument the `CCNode` that made the call, and one that does not. Respectively these are: `CCCallFuncN` (with a `callfuncN_ selector`), and `CCCallFunc` (with a `callfunc_selector`), and were both used inside action sequences we just created.

Time to make our game tick!

Okay. We have our main elements in place and are ready to add the final bit of logic to run the game. But how will everything work?

We will use a system of countdowns to add new meteors and new health packs, as well as a countdown that will incrementally make the game harder to play.

On touch, the player will start the game, if the game is not running, and also add bombs and explode them during gameplay. An explosion creates a shockwave.

On `update`, we will check for a collision between our `_shockwave` sprite (if visible) and all our falling objects. And that's it. Cocos2d-x will take care of all of the rest through our created actions and callbacks!

So let's implement our touch events first.

Time for action – handling touches

It's time to bring the player to our party.

1. Time to implement our `ccTouchesBegan` method. We'll begin by handling the two game states, `intro` and `game over`:

```
void GameLayer::ccTouchesBegan
    (CCSet* pTouches, CCEvent* event) {

    //if game not running, we are seeing either intro or
    //gameover
    if (!_running) {
      //if intro, hide intro message
      if (_introMessage->isVisible()) {
        _introMessage->setVisible(false);

        //if game over, hide game over message
      } else if (_gameOverMessage->isVisible()) {
        SimpleAudioEngine::sharedEngine()->stopAllEffects();
        _gameOverMessage->setVisible(false);

      }

      this->resetGame();
      return;
    }
```

2. Here we check to see if the game is running. If it is not, we check to see if any of our messages are visible. If `_introMessage` is visible we hide it. If `_gameOverMessage` is visible, we stop all current sound effects and hide the message as well. Then we call a method called `resetGame`, which will reset all of the game data (energy, score, and countdowns) to their initial values and then set `_running` to `true`.

3. Next we handle the touches. We only need to handle one each time so we use `->anyObject()` on our `CCSet`:

```
CCTouch *touch = (CCTouch *)pTouches->anyObject();

if (touch) {

  //if bomb already growing...
  if (_bomb->isVisible()) {
    //stop all actions on bomb, halo and sparkle
    _bomb->stopAllActions();
    CCSprite * child;
    child = (CCSprite *) _bomb->getChildByTag(kSpriteHalo);
```

```
      child->stopAllActions();
      child = (CCSprite *) _bomb
      ->getChildByTag(kSpriteSparkle);
      child->stopAllActions();

      //if bomb is the right size, then create shockwave
      if (_bomb->getScale() > 0.3f) {
        _shockWave->setScale(0.1f);
        _shockWave->setPosition(_bomb->getPosition());
        _shockWave->setVisible(true);
        _shockWave->runAction(CCScaleTo::create(0.5f, _bomb
        ->getScale() * 2.0f));
        _shockWave->runAction((CCFiniteTimeAction*)
        _shockwaveSequence->copy()->autorelease());
        SimpleAudioEngine::sharedEngine()
        ->playEffect("bombRelease.wav");

      } else {
        SimpleAudioEngine::sharedEngine()
        ->playEffect("bombFail.wav");
      }
      _bomb->setVisible(false);
      //reset hits with shockwave, so we can count combo hits
      _shockwaveHits = 0;

      //if no bomb currently on screen, create one
    } else {
      CCPoint tap = touch->getLocation();
      _bomb->stopAllActions();
      _bomb->setScale(0.1f);
      _bomb->setPosition(tap);
      _bomb->setVisible(true);
      _bomb->setOpacity(50);
      _bomb->runAction((CCAction *) _growBomb->copy()
      ->autorelease());

      CCSprite * child;
      child = (CCSprite *) _bomb->getChildByTag(kSpriteHalo);
      child->runAction((CCAction *) _rotateSprite->copy()
      ->autorelease());
      child = (CCSprite *) _bomb
      ->getChildByTag(kSpriteSparkle);
      child->runAction((CCAction *) _rotateSprite->copy()
      ->autorelease());
    }
  }
```

4. If _bomb is visible, it means it's already growing on the screen. So on touch, we use the `stopAllActions()` method on the bomb and we use the `stopAllActions()` method on its children, which we retrieve through our tags:

```
child = (CCSprite *) _bomb->getChildByTag(kSpriteHalo);
child->stopAllActions();
child = (CCSprite *) _bomb->getChildByTag(kSpriteSparkle);
child->stopAllActions();
```

5. If the _bomb is the right size, we start our _shockwave. If it is not the right size, we play a bomb failure sound effect; there is no explosion and _shockwave is not made visible.

6. If we have an explosion, then the _shockwave sprite is set to 10 percent of the scale, it's placed at the same spot as the bomb, and we run a couple of actions on it: we grow the _shockwave to twice the scale that the bomb was when it went off, and we run a copy of our _shockwaveSequence that we created earlier.

7. Finally, if no _bomb is currently visible on screen then we create one. Then we run copies of previously-created actions on the _bomb and its children. When the _bomb grows, its children also grow. But when the children rotate, the bomb does not: a parent changes its children, but the children do not change their parent.

What just happened?

We just added part of the core logic of the game. It is with touches that the player creates and explodes bombs to stop meteors from reaching the city. Now we need to create our falling objects. But first, let's set up our countdowns and our game data.

Time for action – starting and restarting the game

Let's add the logic to start or restart the game.

1. Let's write the implementation for `resetGame`:

```
void GameLayer::resetGame(void) {
    _score = 0;
    _energy = 100;

    //reset timers and "speeds"
    _meteorInterval = 2.5;
    _meteorTimer = _meteorInterval * 0.99f;
    _meteorSpeed = 10;//in seconds to reach ground
    _healthInterval = 20;
    _healthTimer = 0;
```

```
_healthSpeed = 15;//in seconds to reach ground

_difficultyInterval = 60;
_difficultyTimer = 0;

_running = true;

//reset labels
CCString * value = CCString::createWithFormat
("%i%s", _energy, "%");
_energyDisplay->setString(value->getCString());

value = CCString::createWithFormat("%i", _score);
_scoreDisplay->setString(value->getCString());
}
```

2. Next, add the implementation of stopGame:

```
void GameLayer::stopGame() {

    _running = false;

    //stop all actions currently running
    int count = _fallingObjects->count();

    CCSprite * sprite;
    for (int i = count-1; i >= 0; i--) {
      sprite = (CCSprite *) _fallingObjects->objectAtIndex(i);
      sprite->stopAllActions();
      sprite->setVisible(false);
      _fallingObjects->removeObjectAtIndex(i);
    }
    if (_bomb->isVisible()) {
      _bomb->stopAllActions();
      _bomb->setVisible(false);
      CCSprite * child;
      child = (CCSprite *) _bomb->getChildByTag(kSpriteHalo);
      child->stopAllActions();
      child = (CCSprite *) _bomb
      ->getChildByTag(kSpriteSparkle);
      child->stopAllActions();
    }
    if (_shockWave->isVisible()) {
      _shockWave->stopAllActions();
      _shockWave->setVisible(false);
    }

}
```

What just happened?

With these methods we can control the game play. We start the game with default values through `resetGame()`, and we stop all actions with `stopGame()`.

Already implemented in the class is the method that makes the game more difficult as time progresses. If you take a look at the method (`increaseDifficulty`) you will see that it reduces the interval between meteors, and reduces the time it takes for meteors to reach the ground.

All we need now is the `update` method to run the countdowns and check for collisions.

Time for action – updating the game

We already have the code that updates the countdowns inside `update`. If it's time to add a meteor or a health pack we do it. If it's time to make the game more difficult to play, we do that too.

It is possible to use an action for these timers: a CCSequence with a CCDelay action object and a callback. But there are advantages to using these countdowns. It's easier to reset them and to change them, and we can take them right into our main loop.

So it's time to add our main loop.

1. What we need to do is check for collisions. So add the following code:

```
int count;
CCSprite * sprite;

//check collision with shockwave
if (_shockWave->isVisible()) {
  count = _fallingObjects->count();

  for (int i = count-1; i >= 0; i--) {
    sprite = (CCSprite *) _fallingObjects->objectAtIndex(i);
    float diffx = _shockWave->getPositionX() - sprite
    ->getPositionX();
    float diffy = _shockWave->getPositionY() - sprite
    ->getPositionY();

    if (pow(diffx, 2) + pow(diffy, 2) <= pow
    (_shockWave->boundingBox().size.width * 0.5f, 2)) {
      sprite->stopAllActions();
      sprite->runAction((CCAction *) _explosion->copy()
      ->autorelease());
```

```
      SimpleAudioEngine::sharedEngine()
      ->playEffect("boom.wav");
      if (sprite->getTag() == kSpriteMeteor) {
        _shockwaveHits++;
        _score += _shockwaveHits * 13 + _shockwaveHits * 2;
      }
      //play sound
      _fallingObjects->removeObjectAtIndex(i);
    }
  }

  CCString * value = CCString::createWithFormat
  ("%i", _score);
  _scoreDisplay->setString(value->getCString());
}
```

2. If `_shockwave` is visible, we check the distance between it and each sprite in `_fallingObjects` CCArray. If we hit any meteor, we increase the value of the `_shockwaveHits` property so we can award the player for multiple hits. Next we move the clouds:

```
//move clouds
count = _clouds->count();
for (int i = 0; i < count; i++) {
  sprite = (CCSprite *) _clouds->objectAtIndex(i);
  sprite->setPositionX(sprite->getPositionX() + dt * 20);
  if (sprite->getPositionX() > _screenSize.width + sprite
  ->boundingBox().size.width * 0.5f) {
    sprite->setPositionX(-sprite->boundingBox().size.width *
    0.5f);
  }
}
```

3. I chose not to use a CCMoveTo action for the clouds, in order to show you the amount of code that can be replaced by a simple action. If not for Cocos2d-x actions, we would have to implement logic to move, rotate, swing, scale, and explode all our sprites!

   And finally add the following code snippet:

```
if (_bomb->isVisible()) {
  if (_bomb->getScale() > 0.3f) {
    if (_bomb->getOpacity() != 255)
    _bomb->setOpacity(255);
  }
}
```

4. We give the player an extra visual cue as to when a bomb is ready to explode, by changing its opacity.

What just happened?

The main loop is pretty straightforward when you don't have to worry about updating individual sprites, as our actions take care of that for us. We pretty much only need to run collision checks between our sprites, and to determine when it's time to throw something new at the player.

So now the only thing left to do is grab the meteors and health packs from the pools when their timers are up. So let's get right to it.

Time for action – retrieving objects from the pool

We just need to use the correct index to retrieve the objects from their respective arrays.

1. To retrieve meteor sprites, we'll use the `resetMeteor` method:

```
void GameLayer::resetMeteor(void) {

    //if too many objects on screen, return
    if (_fallingObjects->count() > 30) return;

    CCSprite * meteor = (CCSprite *) _meteorPool
    ->objectAtIndex(_meteorPoolIndex);
    _meteorPoolIndex++;
    if (_meteorPoolIndex == _meteorPool->count())
    _meteorPoolIndex = 0;

    //pick start and target positions for new meteor
    int meteor_x = rand() % (int) (_screenSize.width * 0.8f) +
    _screenSize.width * 0.1f;
    int meteor_target_x = rand() % (int)
    (_screenSize.width * 0.8f) + _screenSize.width * 0.1f;

    meteor->stopAllActions();
    meteor->setPosition(ccp(meteor_x, _screenSize.height +
    meteor->boundingBox().size.height * 0.5));

    //create action for meteor
    CCActionInterval*  rotate = CCRotateBy::create
    (0.5f ,  -90);
    CCAction*  repeatRotate = CCRepeatForever::create
    ( rotate );
    CCFiniteTimeAction*  sequence = CCSequence::create(
    CCMoveTo::create(_meteorSpeed, ccp
    (meteor_target_x, _screenSize.height * 0.15f)),
    CCCallFuncN::create
    (this, callfuncN_selector(GameLayer::fallingObjectDone)),
```

```
                    NULL);

         meteor->setVisible ( true );
         meteor->runAction(repeatRotate);
         meteor->runAction(sequence);
         _fallingObjects->addObject(meteor);

      }
```

2. We grab the next available meteor from the pool, then we pick a random start and end x value for its CCMoveTo action. The meteor starts at the top of the screen and will move to the bottom towards the city, but the x value is randomly picked each time.

3. We rotate the meteor inside a CCRepeatForever, and we use a CCSequence to move the sprite to its target position and then callback fallingObjectDone when the meteor has reached its target. We finish by adding the new meteor that we retrieved from the pool to the _fallingObjects array, so we can check collisions with it.

4. The method to retrieve the health (resetHealth) sprites is pretty much the same, only with the swingHealth action used instead of rotate. You'll find that method already implemented in GameLayer.cpp.

What just happened?

In resetGame we set the timers, and we update them in the update method. We use these timers to add meteors and health packs to the screen by grabbing the next available one from their respective pool, and then we proceed to run collision between an exploding bomb and these falling objects.

Notice that in both resetMeteor and resetHealth we don't add new sprites if too many are on the screen already.

```
    if ( _fallingObjects->count() > 30) return;
```

This way the game does not get ridiculously hard, and we never run out of unused objects in our pools.

And the very last bit of logic in our game is our fallingObjectDone callback, called when either a meteor or a health pack has reached the ground, at which point it awards or punishes the player for letting sprites through.

When you take a look at that method inside GameLayer.cpp, you will notice how we use ->getTag() to quickly ascertain which type of sprite we are dealing with (the one calling the method).

```
    if (pSender->getTag() == kSpriteMeteor) {
```

If it's a meteor, we decrease energy from the player, play a sound effect, and run the explosion animation; this is an autorelease copy of the _groundHit action that we retained earlier, so we don't need to repeat all that logic every time we need to run this action.

If the item is a health pack, we either increase the energy or give the player some points; play a nice sound effect; and hide the sprite.

Play the game!

We've been coding like mad, and it's finally time to run the game. But first, don't forget to release all of the items that we retained. In GameLayer.cpp, add our destructor method:

```
GameLayer::~GameLayer () {

    //release all retained actions
    CC_SAFE_RELEASE(_growBomb);
    CC_SAFE_RELEASE(_rotateSprite);
    CC_SAFE_RELEASE(_shockwaveSequence);
    CC_SAFE_RELEASE(_swingHealth);
    CC_SAFE_RELEASE(_groundHit);
    CC_SAFE_RELEASE(_explosion);

    //release all retained arrays
    CC_SAFE_RELEASE(_clouds);
    CC_SAFE_RELEASE(_meteorPool);
    CC_SAFE_RELEASE(_healthPool);
    CC_SAFE_RELEASE(_fallingObjects);
}
```

Once again, you may refer to `7341_04_FINAL_PROJECT.zip` if you find any problems running the code.

And as a bonus, I've added another version of the game with an extra type of enemy to deal with: a UFO hell bent on zapping the city! You can find this in `7341_04_BONUS_PROJECT.zip`.

Pop quiz – sprites and actions

Q 1. A `CCSpriteBatchNode` can contain what types of elements?

1.   Sprites using textures from two or more sprite sheets.
2.   Sprites using the same source texture.
3.   Blank sprites.
4.   Sprites using texture from one sprite sheet and one other image.

Q 2. In order to run an action non-stop, I need to use:

1.   `CCRepeatForever`.
2.   `CCRepeat`.
3.   The default behavior of an action is to run non-stop.
4.   Actions can't repeat forever.

Q 3. In order to animate a sprite so that it would move to a certain point on the screen and then fade out, I would need what actions?

1.   A `CCSequence` listing a `CCEaseIn` and a `CCEaseOut` action.
2.   A `CCSequence` listing a `CCFadeOut` and a `CCMoveTo` action.
3.   A `CCSequence` listing a `CCMoveTo` or `CCMoveBy` and a `CCFadeOut` action.
4.   A `CCSequence` listing a `CCRotateBy` and a `CCFadeOut`.

Q 4. To create a sprite frame animation what group of classes are absolutely essential?

1.   `CCSprite, CCSpriteBatchNode, CCEaseIn`.
2.   `CCSpriteFrameCache, CCRotateBy, CCActionManager`.
3.   `CCSprite, CCLayer, CCFadeOut`.
4.   `CCSpriteFrame, CCAnimation, CCAnimate`.

Summary

In my opinion, after `CCNodes` and all its derived objects, `CCActions` are the second best thing about Cocos2d-x. They are time savers, and can quickly spice things up in any project with professional looking animations. And I hope that with the examples found in this chapter, along with the ones found in the Cocos2d-x samples test project, you will be able to create any action you need with Cocos2d-x.

In the next chapter I'll introduce you to another simple thing you can use to spice things up in your game: particles!

5
On the Line – Rocket Through

In our third game, Rocket Through, we'll use particle effects to spice things up a bit, and we'll use CCNode *to make our own OpenGL drawings on the screen. And be advised, this game uses quite a bit of vector math, but luckily for us, Cocos2d-x comes bundled with a sweet pack of helper methods to deal with that as well.*

You will learn:

- How to load and setup a particle system
- How to draw primitives (lines, circles, and more) on a CCNode
- How to use the vector math helper methods included in Cocos2d-x

The game – Rocket Through

In this sci-fi version of the classic Snake game engine, you control a rocket ship that must move around seven planets collecting tiny supernovas. But here's the catch: you can only steer the rocket by rotating it around pivot points put in place through touch events. So the vector of movement we set for the rocket ship is at times linear and at times circular.

The game settings

This is a universal game designed for the regular iPad and then scaled up and down to match the screen resolution of other devices. It is set to play in portrait mode and it does not support multi-touches.

Play first, work later

Download the `7341_05_START_PROJECT.zip` and `7341_05_FINAL_PROJECT.zip` files from this book's support page.

You will once again use the **Start Project** option to work on; this way you won't need to type logic or syntax already covered in previous chapters. The **Start Project** option contains all of the resource files, and all the classes declarations, as well as place-holders for all of the methods inside the classes' implementation files. We'll go over these in a moment.

You should **Run** the Final Project version to acquaint yourself with the game: By pressing and dragging your finger on the rocket ship you draw a line. Release the touch and you create a pivot point. The ship will rotate around this pivot point until you press again on the ship to release it. Your aim is to collect the bright supernovas and avoid the planets.

The start project

If you run the **Start Project** option you should see that the basic game screen is already in place. There is no need to repeat the steps we've taken in our previous tutorial for creating a batch node and positioning all the screen sprites. We once again have a `_gameBatchNode` object and a `createGameScreen` method.

By all means read through the code inside the `createGameScreen` method. Of key importance here is that each planet we create is stored inside `_planets` CCArray. We also create our `_rocket` object (class `Rocket`) and our `_lineContainer` object (`LineContainer` class) here. More on these soon.

In the **Start Project** option, we also have our old friend GameSprite, which here extends CCSprite with an extra method to get the radius() method of our sprites. The Rocket object and all of the planets are GameSprite objects.

Screen settings

Assuming that you have the **Start Project** option opened in Xcode, let's review the screen settings for this game in AppDelegate.cpp, where inside the applicationDidFinishLaunching method you should see this:

```
CCSize designSize = CCSize(768, 1024);

CCEGLView::sharedOpenGLView()->setDesignResolutionSize(designSize.
width, designSize.height, kResolutionExactFit);

float screenRatio = screenSize.height / screenSize.width;

if (screenSize.width > 768) {
    CCFileUtils::sharedFileUtils()->setResourceDirectory("ipadhd");
    pDirector->
    setContentScaleFactor(screenSize.height/designSize.height);
    } else if (screenSize.width > 320) {
    if (screenRatio >= 1.5f) {
    CCFileUtils::sharedFileUtils()->setResourceDirectory("iphonehd");
    } else {
        CCFileUtils::sharedFileUtils()->setResourceDirectory("ipad");
    }
    pDirector-
    >setContentScaleFactor(screenSize.height/designSize.height);
    } else {
    CCFileUtils::sharedFileUtils()->setResourceDirectory("iphone");
    pDirector-
    >setContentScaleFactor(screenSize.height/designSize.height);
}
```

We start the same way as we did in the previous game. Only this time the game was designed for the regular iPad. The other difference here is the extra folder called **iphonehd**.

This is yet another technique when planning a game for multiple devices. The iPad is the oddball in terms of screen size: it has a 1.33 screen ratio (longer side divided by shorter side). Most Android devices will range between 1.6 and 1.77, with a few sharing the iPhone screen ratio of 1.5.

Why should you care? In this game most sprites are circles and the difference in screen ratio would cause them to look squished when ported to different screens using the `kResolutionExactFit` parameter, which distorts your game screen to fit the screen of the device.

There are a dozen ways to deal with this; you could, for instance, give preference for the iPhone ratio when designing your game, as it's much closer to the average screen ratio out there, and then use `kResolutionShowAll` instead of `kResolutionExactFit`. This would show borders around the screen in ratios different than 1.5, but would not deform the sprites (we'll use this method in *Chapter 8, Getting Physical: Box2D*).

But here I used another method, I created sprite sheets that account for the squished look of the sprites in different screen ratios, counteracting the distortion. You, or your designer, could produce art for different screen ratios, such as 1.3, 1.5, 1.6, and 1.7, and pack different sets of images for different device families. For the Apple family, the solution shown here works very well and we can use the entire screen through `kResolutionExactFit`.

The following image shows two sets of images found in the sprite sheets. Notice the distortion in the iPhone ones. In the actual game this distortion will disappear as it will counteract the change from a 1.3 screen ratio to a 1.5:

IPAD   **IPHONE**

So what are particles?

Particles, or **particle systems**, are a way to add special effects to your applications. In general terms this is achieved by the use of a large number of tiny textured sprites (particles), which are animated and run through a series of transformations. You can use these systems to create smoke, explosions, sparks, lightning, rain, snow, and other such effects.

As I mentioned in the first chapter, you should seriously consider getting yourself a program to help you design your particle systems. In this game, the particles were created in `ParticleDesigner`.

It's time to add them to our game.

Time for action – creating particle systems

For particles, all we need is the XML file describing the particle system's properties:

1. Let's go to `GameLayer.cpp`.

2. The game initializes by calling `createGameScreen`, which is already in place, then calls `createParticles` and `createStarGrid`, which are also implemented. So let's go over the `createParticles` method now.

3. Go to that method in `GameLayer.cpp` and add this code:

```
_jet = CCParticleSystemQuad::create("jet.plist");
_jet->setSourcePosition(ccp(-_rocket->getRadius() * 0.8f,0));
_jet->setAngle(180);
_jet->stopSystem();
this->addChild(_jet, kBackground);

_boom = CCParticleSystemQuad::create("boom.plist");
_boom->stopSystem();
this->addChild(_boom, kForeground);

_comet = CCParticleSystemQuad::create("comet.plist");
_comet->stopSystem();
_comet->setPosition(ccp(0, _screenSize.height * 0.6f));
_comet->setVisible(false);
this->addChild(_comet, kForeground);

_pickup = CCParticleSystemQuad::create("plink.plist");
_pickup->stopSystem();
this->addChild(_pickup, kMiddleground);

_warp = CCParticleSystemQuad::create("warp.plist");
_warp->setPosition(_rocket->getPosition());
this->addChild(_warp, kBackground);

_star = CCParticleSystemQuad::create("star.plist");
_star->stopSystem();
_star->setVisible(false);
this->addChild(_star, kBackground, kSpriteStar);
```

What just happened?

We created our first particles. `ParticleDesigner` exports the particle system data as a `plist` file, which we used to create our `CCParticleSystemQuad` objects. You should open one of these files in Xcode to review the number of settings used in a particle system. From Cocos2d-x you can modify any of these settings through setters inside `CCParticleSystem`.

The particles we'll use in this game are:

◆ The first one, `_jet`, is attached to the `_rocket` object and will trail behind the `_rocket` object. We set the system's angle and source position parameters to match the `_rocket` sprite.

◆ `_boom` is the particle system used when `_rocket` explodes.

◆ `_comet` is a particle system that moves across the screen at set intervals and can collide with `_rocket`.

◆ `_pickup` is used when a star is collected.

◆ `_warp` marks the initial position of the rocket.

◆ `_star` is the particle system used for the star the rocket must collect.

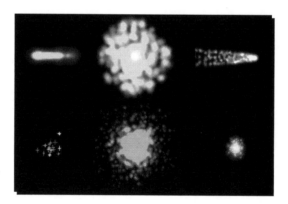

All particle systems are added as children to `GameLayer`; they cannot be added to our `CCSpriteBatchNode`. And you must call `stopSystem()` on each system as they're created; otherwise they will start playing as soon as they are added to a node.

In order to run the system you make a call to `resetSystem()`.

 Cocos2d-x comes bundled with some common particle systems that you can modify for your own needs. If you go to the test folder at: `samples/TestCpp/Classes/ParticleTest` you will see examples of these systems being used. The actual particles data files are found at: `samples/TestCpp/Resources/Particles`

Creating the grid

Let's take some time now to review the grid logic in the game. This grid is created inside the createStarGrid method in GameLayer.cpp. What the method does is determine all of the possible spots on the screen where we can place the _star particle system.

We use a C++ vector list called _grid to store the available spots, as it will be easier to shuffle the list this way than to use CCArray:

```
std::vector<CCPoint> _grid;
```

The method divides the screen into multiple cells of 32 x 32 pixels, ignoring the areas too close to the screen borders (gridFrame). Then we check the distance between each cell and the planet sprites stored inside CCArray _planets. If the cell is far enough from the planets we store it inside the _grid vector as CCPoint.

In the following image you can get an idea of the result we're after. We do not want any of the white cells overlapping any of the planets.

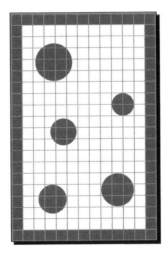

We output a message to the console with CCLog stating how many cells we end up with:

```
CCLog("POSSIBLE STARS: %i", _grid.size());
```

This vector list will be shuffled at each new game, so we end up with a random sequence of possible positions for our star:

```
std::random_shuffle(_grid.begin(), _grid.end());
```

This way we never place a star on top of a planet or too close to it that the rocket could not reach it without colliding with the planet.

Drawing primitives in Cocos2d-x

One of the main elements in the game is the `LineContainer.cpp` class. It is a CCNode derived class that allows us to draw lines and circles on the screen.

Every CCNode has a `draw` method which is implemented inside all of its subclasses. This is where the OpenGL drawing of our sprites take place, and it gets called automatically by the framework during rendering (so up to 60 times a second).

So in order to draw something yourself, you just need to override this method; and then in order to draw primitives, you use the helper methods from a Cocos2d-x class called `CCDrawingPrimitives.cpp`.

The methods we'll use are: `ccDrawLine` and `ccDrawCircle`.

Time for action – let's do some drawing!

It's time to implement the drawing inside `LineContainer.cpp`. You will notice that this class already has most of its methods implemented, so you can save a little typing. I'll go over what these methods represent once we add the game's main update method, but basically `LineContainer` will be used to display the lines that the player draws on screen in order to manipulate `_rocket` sprite, as well as display an energy bar that acts as a sort of timer in our game:

1. What we need to change here is the draw method we inherited from CCNode. So this is what you need to type inside that method:

```
switch (_lineType) {
    case LINE_NONE:
        break;
    case LINE_TEMP:

        ccDrawColor4F(1.0, 1.0, 1.0, 1.0);
        ccDrawLine(_tip, _pivot);
        ccDrawCircle(_pivot, 10, CC_DEGREES_TO_RADIANS(360),
        10, false);

        break;

    case LINE_DASHED:
        ccDrawColor4F(1.0, 1.0, 1.0, 1.0);
        ccDrawCircle(_pivot, 10, M_PI, 10, false);

        int segments = _lineLength / (_dash + _dashSpace);

        float t = 0.0f;
```

```
float x_;
float y_;

for (int i = 0; i < segments + 1; i++) {

    x_ = _pivot.x + t * (_tip.x - _pivot.x);
    y_ = _pivot.y + t * (_tip.y - _pivot.y);

    ccDrawCircle(ccp ( x_, y_ ), 4, M_PI, 6, false);

    t += (float) 1 / segments;
}
break;
}
```

2. We end our draw method by drawing the energy bar in the same
    `LineContainer` node:

```
ccDrawColor4F(0.0, 0.0, 0.0, 1.0);
ccDrawLine(ccp(_energyLineX, _screenSize.height * 0.1f),
    ccp(_energyLineX, _screenSize.height * 0.9f));
ccDrawColor4F(1.0, 0.5, 0.0, 1.0);
ccDrawLine(ccp(_energyLineX, _screenSize.height * 0.1f),
    ccp(_energyLineX, _screenSize.height * 0.1f + _energy *
_energyHeight ));
```

What just happened?

You just learned how to override the draw method of CCNodes to add your own drawings.
The process is remarkably simple because inside every ccDraw method Cocos2d-x is taking
care of all the grunt work of dealing with OpenGL commands and vertices.

In LineContainer we use a switch statement to determine how to draw the player's line.
If the _lineType property is set to LINE_NONE we don't draw anything (this will in effect
clear the screen of any drawings done by the player).

If _lineType is LINE_TEMP this means that the player is currently dragging a finger away
from the _rocket object and we want to show a white line from the _rocket current
position to the player's current touch position. These points are called, respectively, tip
and pivot.

We also draw a circle directly on the pivot point.

```
ccDrawColor4F(1.0, 1.0, 1.0, 1.0);//set draw color to white
ccDrawLine(_tip, _pivot);
ccDrawCircle(_pivot, 10, CC_DEGREES_TO_RADIANS(360), 10, false);
```

`ccDrawColor4F` sets the color in RGB values and the opacity of the next thing to be drawn on the screen.

A circle is actually a series of lines drawn around a point. So with `ccDrawCircle` here we are drawing a full circle on the `_pivot` point, with a radius of 10 pixels and with 10 segments (lines). The last `boolean` value states whether or not we want a line drawn to the center of the circle.

If `_lineType` is `LINE_DASHED` then this means that the player has removed his or her finger from the screen and set a new pivot point for the `_rocket` to rotate around. We draw a white dotted line, using what is known as the bezier linear formula to draw a series of tiny circles from the `_rocket`'s current position and the pivot point:

```
for (int i = 0; i < segments + 1; i++) {

    x_ = _pivot.x + t * (_tip.x - _pivot.x);
    y_ = _pivot.y + t * (_tip.y - _pivot.y);

    ccDrawCircle(ccp ( x_, y_ ), 4, M_PI, 6, false);
    t += (float) 1 / segments;
}
```

And finally, for the energy bar we draw a black line underneath an orange one. The orange one resizes as the value for `_energy` in `LineContainer` is reduced. The black one stays the same and is there to show contrast. You layer your drawings through the order of the `ccDraw` calls you make; so the first things drawn appear underneath the latter ones.

One curious point here: take a look at the constructor in `LineContainer.cpp`. We make a call there to set the line width that we are going to use in every call to `ccDraw`:

```
glLineWidth(8.0 * CC_CONTENT_SCALE_FACTOR());
```

But notice that this value does not get scaled by the framework. Whenever you have a value that does not get scaled, you must add the logic yourself, multiplying the value by `CC_CONTENT_SCALE_FACTOR()`, which, if you recall, gets set in `AppDelegate.cpp`.

The Rocket sprite

Time to tackle the second object in the game: the rocket.

Once again I already put in place the part of the logic that's old news to you. But please review the code already inside `Rocket.cpp`. We have a method for resetting the rocket every time a new game starts (`reset`), and a method to show the selected state of the rocket (`select(bool flag)`) by changing its displayed texture:

```
if (flag) {
    this->setDisplayFrame(CCSpriteFrameCache::sharedSpriteFrameCac
he()->spriteFrameByName("rocket_on.png"));
} else {
    this->setDisplayFrame(CCSpriteFrameCache::sharedSpriteFrameCac
he()->spriteFrameByName("rocket.png"));
}
```

This will either show the rocket with a glow around it, or not.

And finally, we have a method to check collision with the sides of the screen (`collidedWithSides`). If there is a collision we adjust the rocket so that it moves away from the screen side that it collided with and we release it from any pivot point.

What we really need to worry about here is the rocket's update method. And that's what we'll add next.

Time for action – updating our Rocket

The game's main loop will call the rocket's `update` method in every iteration:

1. Inside the empty `update` method in `Rocket.cpp` add these lines:

    ```
    CCPoint position = this->getPosition();

    if (_rotationOrientation == ROTATE_NONE) {
        position.x += _vector.x * dt;
        position.y += _vector.y * dt;

    } else {

        //rotate point around a pivot by a certain amount
        CCPoint rotatedPoint = ccpRotateByAngle(position, _pivot,
    _angularSpeed * dt);

        position.x = rotatedPoint.x;
        position.y = rotatedPoint.y;

        float rotatedAngle;
    ```

```
        CCPoint clockwise = ccpRPerp( ccpSub(position, _pivot) );

        if (_rotationOrientation == ROTATE_COUNTER) {
            rotatedAngle = atan2 (-1 * clockwise.y, -1 * clockwise.x);
        } else {
            rotatedAngle = atan2 (clockwise.y, clockwise.x);
        }


        //update rocket vector
        _vector.x = _speed * cos (rotatedAngle);
        _vector.y = _speed * sin (rotatedAngle);

        this->setRotationFromVector();

        if (this->getRotation() > 0) {
            this->setRotation( fmodf(this->getRotation(), 360.0f)
            );
        } else {
            this->setRotation( fmodf(this->getRotation(), -360.0f)
            );
        }
    }
```

2. Here we are saying that if the rocket is not rotating (`_rotationOrientation == ROTATE_NONE`) then we just move it according to its current `_vector`. If it is rotating then we use the Cocos2d-x helper `ccpRotateByAngle` method to find its next position around its pivot point:

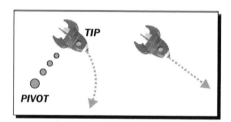

3. The method will rotate any point around a pivot by a certain angle. So we rotate the rocket's updated position around its pivot (determined by the player) by using a property of `Rocket` called `_angularSpeed`; we'll see in a moment how it gets calculated.

4. Based on whether the rocket is rotating clockwise or counterclockwise, we adjust its rotation so the rocket will be at a 90 degree angle with the line drawn between the rocket and its pivot point. Then we change the rocket's movement vector based on this rotated angle, and we wrap the value of that angle between 0 and 360.

5. Finish up the `update` method with these lines:

```
if (_targetRotation > this->getRotation() + 180) {
    _targetRotation -= 360;
}
if (_targetRotation < this->getRotation() - 180) {
    _targetRotation += 360;
}

this->setPosition(position);

_dr = _targetRotation - this->getRotation();
_ar = _dr * _rotationSpring;
_vr += _ar ;
_vr *= _rotationDamping;
m_fRotation += _vr ;
```

6. With these lines we determine the new target rotation of our sprite and we run an animation to rotate the rocket to its target rotation (with a bit of a spring to it). We use the `m_fRotation` property from `CCNode` here to adjust the sprite's rotation.

> Be careful when using the protected properties from `CCNode` instead of setters. Usually the setters will change a `dirty` property of `CCNodes` to true, meaning that the sprite must be redrawn because it has changed since its last render. Changing the property value might not change the value of `dirty`, meaning that you don't get to see the change.

What just happened?

We just wrote the logic that will move the rocket around the screen, whether the rocket is rotating or not.

So when the player picks a pivot point for the `_rocket` sprite, this pivot point is passed to both `Rocket` and `LineContainer`. The former will use it to rotate it's vector around it and the later will use it to draw a dotted line between `_rocket` and the pivot point.

> We can't use `CCAction` to rotate the sprite because the target rotation is updated too many times in our logic and `CCAction` needs time to initialize and run.

So it's time to code the touch events to make all of that logic fall into place.

Time for Action – handling touches

We need to implement ccTouchesBegan, ccTouchesMoved, and ccTouchesEnded:

1. In GameLayer.cpp, inside ccTouchesBegan add these lines:

```
if (!_running) return;

CCTouch *touch = (CCTouch *)pTouches->anyObject();

if (touch) {

    CCPoint tap = touch->getLocation();

    //track if tapping on ship
    float dx = _rocket->getPositionX() - tap.x;
    float dy = _rocket->getPositionY() - tap.y;

    if (dx * dx + dy * dy <= pow(_rocket->getRadius() * 1.2, 2)
    ) {
        //clear lines
        _lineContainer->setLineType ( LINE_NONE );
        _rocket->setRotationOrientation ( ROTATE_NONE );
        _drawing = true;
    }
}
```

When a touch begins, we only need to determine if it's touching the ship, if it is we set our _drawing property to true. This will indicate that we have a valid point (one that began by touching the _rocket).

2. We clear any lines we may be currently drawing in _lineContainer by calling setLineType(LINE_NONE), and we make sure that_rocket will not rotate until we have a pivot point, by releasing _rocket (setRotationOrientation (ROTATE_NONE)) so it will continue to move on its current linear trajectory (_vector).

3. From here we begin drawing a new line, with the next ccTouchesMoved method. Inside that method, we add these lines:

```
if (!_running) return;

if (_drawing) {

    CCTouch *touch = (CCTouch *)pTouches->anyObject();

    if(touch ) {
```

```
CCPoint tap = touch->getLocation();

float dx = _rocket->getPositionX() - tap.x;
float dy = _rocket->getPositionY() - tap.y;

if (dx * dx + dy * dy > pow (_minLineLength, 2)) {
    _rocket->select(true);
    _lineContainer->setPivot ( tap );
    _lineContainer->setLineType ( LINE_TEMP );
} else {
    _rocket->select(false);
    _lineContainer->setLineType ( LINE_NONE );
}

}

}
```

4. We'll handle touch moved only if we are using `_drawing`, meaning that the player has pressed on the ship and is now dragging his or her finger across the screen.

   Once the distance between the finger and `_rocket` is greater than the `_minLineLength` that we stipulate in game init, we give a visual cue to the player by adding a glow `around _rocket (_rocket->select(true))` and we draw the new line in `_lineContainer` by passing it the touch's current position and setting line type to `LINE_TEMP`. If the minimum length is not reached we don't show a line nor we show the player selected.

5. Next comes `ccTouchesEnded`. There is logic in place already inside our `ccTouchesEnded` method, which deals with game states. You should uncomment the calls to `resetGame` and add a new `else if` statement inside the method:

```
} else if (_state == kGamePaused) {
    _pauseBtn-
    >setDisplayFrame(CCSpriteFrameCache:
    :sharedSpriteFrameCache()->spriteFrameByName
    ("btn_pause_off.png"));
    _paused->setVisible(false);
    _state = kGamePlay;
    _running = true;
    return;
}
```

6. If the game is paused, we change the texture in the `_pauseBtn` sprite through `CCSprite->setDisplayFrame` and we start running the game again.

7. Now we begin handling the touch. First, we determine if it's landing on the **Pause** button:

```
if (!_running) return;

CCTouch *touch = (CCTouch *)pTouches->anyObject();

if(touch) {

    CCPoint tap = touch->getLocation();

    if (_pauseBtn->boundingBox().containsPoint(tap)) {
        _paused->setVisible(true);
        _state = kGamePaused;
        _pauseBtn-
        >setDisplayFrame(CCSpriteFrameCache:
        :sharedSpriteFrameCache()->spriteFrameByName
        ("btn_pause_on.png"));
        _running = false;
        return;
    }
}
```

8. If so, we change the game state to kGamePaused, change the texture on the _pauseBtn sprite (by retrieving another sprite frame from CCSpriteFrameCache), stop running the game (by pausing it), and return from the function.

9. We can finally make something about the rocket ship. So continuing inside the same if(touch) { conditional seen previously, add the following lines:

```
_drawing = false;
_rocket->select(false);

//if we are showing a temp line
if (_lineContainer->getLineType() == LINE_TEMP) {

    _lineContainer->setPivot (tap);
    _lineContainer->setLineLength ( ccpDistance(_rocket-
    >getPosition(), tap) );

    //set up rocket
    _rocket->setPivot (tap);
```

10. We start by deselecting the _rocket sprite, and then we check to see if we are currently showing a temporary line in _lineContainer. If we are, then this means we can go ahead and create our new pivot point with the player's released touch. We pass that information to _lineContainer with our setPivot method, along with the line length. The _rocket sprite also receives the pivot point information.

Then things get hairy! The _rocket sprite is moving at a pixel-based speed. Once _rocket starts rotating it will move at an angular-based speed, through ccpRotateByAngle. So the next lines are added to translate the current pixel-based speed of _rocket into an angular speed:

```
float circle_length = _lineContainer->getLineLength() * 2 * M_PI;
int iterations = floor(circle_length / _rocket->getSpeed());
_rocket->setAngularSpeed ( 2 * M_PI / iterations);
```

11. The code grabs the length of the circumference about to be described by _rocket (line length * 2 * PI) and divides it by the rocket's speed, getting in return the number of iterations needed for the rocket to complete that length. Then the 360 degrees of the circle is divided by the same number of iterations (but we do it in radians) to arrive at the fraction of a circle that the rocket must rotate at each iteration: its angular speed.

12. What follows next is even more math, using the amazingly helpful methods from Cocos2d-x that are related to vector math (ccpRPerp, ccpDot, ccpSub, to name a few) some of which we've seen already in the Rocket class:

```
CCPoint clockwise = ccpRPerp(ccpSub(_rocket-
>getPosition(), _rocket->getPivot()));

float dot = ccpDot ( clockwise, _rocket->getVector() );

if (dot > 0) {
    _rocket->setAngularSpeed ( _rocket-
    >getAngularSpeed() * -1 );
    _rocket->setRotationOrientation ( ROTATE_CLOCKWISE
    );
    _rocket->setTargetRotation ( CC_RADIANS_TO_DEGREES(
    atan2(clockwise.y, clockwise.x) ) );
    } else {
    _rocket->setRotationOrientation ( ROTATE_COUNTER );
    _rocket->setTargetRotation ( CC_RADIANS_TO_DEGREES
    (atan2(-1 * clockwise.y, -1 * clockwise.x) ) );
}
    _lineContainer->setLineType ( LINE_DASHED );
    }
}
```

13. What they do here is determine in which direction the rocket should rotate, clockwise or counterclockwise, based on its current vector of movement.

14. The line that the player just drew between _rocket and pivot point , which we get by subtracting (ccpSub) those two points, has two perpendicular vectors: one to the right (clockwise) that you get through ccpRPerp and one to the left (counterclockwise) that you get through ccpPerp. We use the angle of one of these vectors as the _rocket's target rotation so the rocket will rotate to be at 90 degrees to the line drawn in LineContainer. And we find the correct perpendicular through the dot product of the _rocket's current vector and one of the perpendiculars (ccpDot).

What just happened?

I know. A lot of math, and all at once! Thankfully, Cocos2d-x made it all much easier to handle.

We just added the logic that allows the player to draw lines and set new pivot points for the _rocket sprite.

The player will steer the _rocket sprite through the planets by giving the rocket a pivot point to rotate around. And by releasing the _rocket from pivot points the player will make it move in a straight line again. All that logic gets managed here in the game's touch events.

And don't worry about the math. If the vector math used in this game looks strange to you, there is *Appendix, Vector Calculations with Cocos2d-x* covering all the logic in greater detail. Understanding how to deal with vectors is a very useful tool in any game developer's toolbox, and Cocos2d-x makes the calculations a breeze.

The game loop

It's time to create our good old ticker! The main loop will be in charge of collision detection, updating the points inside _lineContainer, adjusting our _jet particle system to our _rocket sprite, and a few other things.

Time for action – adding the main loop

Let's implement our main update method:

1. In GameLayer.cpp, inside the update method, add these lines:

```
if (!_running) return;

if (_lineContainer->getLineType() != LINE_NONE) {
    _lineContainer->setTip (_rocket->getPosition() );
```

```
}

//track collision with sides
if (_rocket->collidedWithSides()) {
    _lineContainer->setLineType ( LINE_NONE );
}

_rocket->update(dt);

//update jet particle so it follows rocket
if (!_jet->isActive()) _jet->resetSystem();
_jet->setRotation(_rocket->getRotation());
_jet->setPosition(_rocket->getPosition());
```

We check to see if we are not currently paused. Then, if there is a line for our ship that we need to show in `_lineContainer`, we update the line's tip point with the `_rocket`'s current position.

We run collision checks between `_rocket` and the screen sides, update the `_rocket`, and position and rotate our `_jet` particle system to align it with the `_rocket` sprite.

2. Next we update `_comet` (its countdown, initial position, movement, and collision with `_rocket` if `_comet` is visible):

```
_cometTimer += dt;
float newY;

if (_cometTimer > _cometInterval) {
    _cometTimer = 0;
    if (_comet->isVisible() == false) {
        _comet->setPositionX(0);
        newY =
        (float)rand()/((float)RAND_MAX/_screenSize.height *
        0.6f) + _screenSize.height * 0.2f;
        if (newY > _screenSize.height * 0.9f)
            newY = _screenSize.height * 0.9f;
            _comet->setPositionY(newY);
            _comet->setVisible(true);
            _comet->resetSystem();
    }
}

if (_comet->isVisible()) {
```

```
        //collision with comet
        if (pow(_comet->getPositionX() - _rocket->getPositionX(),
        2) + pow(_comet->getPositionY() - _rocket->getPositionY(),
        2) <= pow (_rocket->getRadius() , 2)) {
            if (_rocket->isVisible()) killPlayer();
        }
        _comet->setPositionX(_comet->getPositionX() + 50 * dt);

        if (_comet->getPositionX() > _screenSize.width * 1.5f) {
            _comet->stopSystem();
            _comet->setVisible(false);
        }
    }
```

3. Next:

```
_lineContainer->update(dt);
_rocket->setOpacity(_lineContainer->getEnergy() * 255);
```

We update _lineContainer, and we slowly reduce the opacity of the _rocket sprite based on the _energy level in _lineContainer. This will add a visual cue for the player that time is running out as the _rocket sprite will slowly turn invisible.

4. Run collision with planets:

```
int count = _planets->count();
GameSprite * planet;
for (int i = 0; i < count; i++) {
    planet = (GameSprite *) _planets->objectAtIndex(i);
    if (pow(planet->getPositionX() - _rocket->getPositionX(),
    2)
    + pow(planet->getPositionY() - _rocket->getPositionY(), 2)
    <=   pow (_rocket->getRadius() * 0.8f + planet->getRadius()
    * 0.65f, 2)) {

        if (_rocket->isVisible()) killPlayer();
        break;
    }
}
```

5. And collision with the star:

```
if (pow(_star->getPositionX() - _rocket->getPositionX(), 2)
    + pow(_star->getPositionY() - _rocket->getPositionY(), 2)
    <=
    pow (_rocket->getRadius() * 1.2f, 2)) {
```

```
_pickup->setPosition(_star->getPosition());
_pickup->resetSystem();
if (_lineContainer->getEnergy() + 0.25f < 1) {
    _lineContainer->setEnergy(_lineContainer->getEnergy() +
    0.25f);
} else {
    _lineContainer->setEnergy(1.0);
}
_rocket->setSpeed(_rocket->getSpeed() + 2);
if (_rocket->getSpeed() > 70) _rocket->setSpeed(70);
    _lineContainer->setEnergyDecrement(0.0002f);
    SimpleAudioEngine::sharedEngine()-
    >playEffect("pickup.wav");
    resetStar();

    int points = 100 - _timeBetweenPickups;
    if (points < 0) points = 0;

    _score += points;
    CCString * value = CCString::createWithFormat("%i",
    _score);
    _scoreDisplay->setString(value->getCString());

    _timeBetweenPickups = 0;
}
```

When we collect _star, we activate the _pickup particle system on the spot
where the _star was, we fill up the player's energy level, we make the game
slightly harder, and we immediately reset _star to its next position, to be collected
again.

The score is based on the time that it took the player to collect the _star.

6. We keep track of this time on the last lines of update where we also check the
energy level:

```
_timeBetweenPickups += dt;
if (_lineContainer->getEnergy() == 0) {
    if (_rocket->isVisible()) killPlayer();
}
```

What just happened?

We added the main loop to our game, and finally have all the pieces talking to each other.
But you probably noticed quite a few calls to methods that we have not implemented yet,
such as killPlayer and resetStar. We'll finish our game logic with these methods.

Kill and reset

It's that time again! Time to kill our player, and reset the game. We also need to move the _star sprite to a new position whenever it is picked up by the player.

Time for action – adding our resets and kills

We need to add logic to restart our game, and to move our pickup star to a new position. But first, let's kill the player:

1. Inside the `killPlayer` method add these lines:

```
void GameLayer::killPlayer() {

    SimpleAudioEngine::sharedEngine()->stopBackgroundMusic();
    SimpleAudioEngine::sharedEngine()->stopAllEffects();
    SimpleAudioEngine::sharedEngine()-
>playEffect("shipBoom.wav");

    //update our particle systems, _boom and _jet
    _boom->setPosition(_rocket->getPosition());
    _boom->resetSystem();
    _rocket->setVisible(false);
    _jet->stopSystem();
    _lineContainer->setLineType ( LINE_NONE );

    _running = false;
    _state = kGameOver;
    _gameOver->setVisible(true);
    _pauseBtn->setVisible(false);
}
```

2. Inside `resetStar` add the following lines of code:

```
void GameLayer::resetStar() {
    CCPoint position = _grid[_gridIndex];
    _gridIndex++;
    if (_gridIndex == _grid.size()) _gridIndex = 0;
    //reset star particles
    _star->setPosition(position);
    _star->setVisible(true);
    _star->resetSystem();
}
```

3. And finally, let's provide our `resetGame` **method:**

```
void GameLayer::resetGame () {

    _rocket->setPosition(ccp(_screenSize.width * 0.5f,
    _screenSize.height * 0.1f));
    _rocket->setOpacity(255);
    _rocket->setVisible(true);
    _rocket->reset();

    _cometInterval = 4;
    _cometTimer = 0;
    _timeBetweenPickups = 0.0;

    _score = 0;
    CCString * value = CCString::createWithFormat("%i",
    _score);
    _scoreDisplay->setString(value->getCString());

    _lineContainer->reset();

    //shuffle grid cells

    std::random_shuffle(_grid.begin(), _grid.end());
    _gridIndex = 0;

    resetStar();

    _warp->stopSystem();

    _running = true;

    SimpleAudioEngine::sharedEngine()-
    >playBackgroundMusic("background.mp3", true);
    SimpleAudioEngine::sharedEngine()->stopAllEffects();
    SimpleAudioEngine::sharedEngine()->playEffect("rocket.wav",
    true);

}
```

Have a go hero

Add logic to the `resetStar` method so that the new position picked is not too close to the `_rocket` sprite. So make the function a recurrent one until a proper position is picked.

You can also take the `warp` particle system, which right now does not do a whole lot, and use it as a random teleport field, so that the rocket may get sucked in by a randomly placed warp, and moved farther away from the target star.

Summary

Congratulations! You now have enough information about Cocos2d-x to produce awesome 2D games. First sprites, then actions, and now particles.

Particles make everything look shiny! They are easy to implement and are a very good way to add an extra bit of animation to your game. But it's very easy to overdo it, so be careful. You don't want to give your players epileptic fits. Also, running too many particles at once could stop your game on its tracks.

In the next chapter we'll see how to use Cocos2d-x to quickly test and develop game ideas.

6

Quick and Easy Sprite – Victorian Rush Hour

In our fourth example of a game built with Cocos2d-x, I'll show you a simple technique for rapid prototyping. Often in game development you want to test the core ideas of your game as soon as possible, because a game may sound fun in your head but in reality it may just not work. Rapid prototyping techniques allow you to test your game as early as possible in the development process as well as build up on the good ideas.

What you'll learn:

♦ How to quickly create placeholder sprites

♦ How to code collision for a platform game

♦ How to create varied terrain for a side-scroller

The game – Victorian Rush Hour

In this game you control a cyclist in Victorian London trying to avoid the traffic on his way home. For reasons no one can explain, he's riding his bike on top of the buildings. As the player, it is your job to ensure he makes it.

The controls are very simple: you tap the screen to make the cyclist jump. While he's in the air, if you tap the screen again the cyclist will open his trusty umbrella, either slowing his descent or adding a boost to his jump.

This game is of a type commonly known as a dash game, a genre that has become increasingly popular online and on various app stores. Usually in these types of games you, the developer, have two choices: either make the terrain the main obstacle and challenge in the game, or make what's added to the terrain be the main challenge (enemies, pick-ups, obstacles, and so on). With this game, I decided on the first option.

So our challenge is to create a game where the terrain is the enemy, but not an unbeatable one.

The game settings

The game is an universal application, designed for the iPad's retina display but with support for other display sizes. It is played in landscape mode and it does not support multi-touch.

Rapid prototyping with Cocos2d-x

The idea behind this is to create sprites as quickly as possible, as placeholders for your game elements, so you can test your game ideas and refine them. Every game in this book was initially developed in the way I'm about to show you, with simple rectangles in place of textured sprites.

The technique shown here allows you to create rectangles of any size and color, to be used in your game logic.

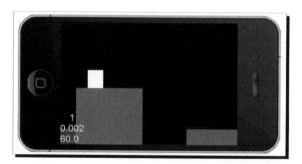

Time for action – creating placeholder sprites

So let me show you how to do that:

Go ahead and download the `7341_06_START_PROJECT.zip` file, if you haven't done so already.

1. When you open the project in Xcode you will see all the classes we'll need for the game, and we'll go over them in a second. But for now just go to `GameLayer.cpp`

2. Scroll down to the last `createGameScreen` method and add these lines:

```
CCSprite * quickSprite = CCSprite::create("blank.png");
quickSprite->setTextureRect(CCRectMake(0, 0, 100, 100));
quickSprite->setColor(ccc3(255,255,255));

quickSprite->setPosition(ccp(_screenSize.width * 0.5, _screenSize.
height * 0.5));
this->addChild(quickSprite);
```

And that's it. The sprite is created with a texture called `blank.png`, which is a 1 x 1 pixel white square you will find in the `Resources` folder. Then we set the size of the sprite's texture rectangle to 100 x 100 pixels (`setTextureRect`), and fill it with a white color (`setColor`). By resizing the texture rectangle we in effect resize the sprite. If you run the game now you should see a white square smack in the middle of the screen.

3. Now delete the lines created in step 2 and replace them with:

```
_gameBatchNode = CCSpriteBatchNode::create("blank.png", 200);
this->addChild(_gameBatchNode, kMiddleground);
```

This creates `_gameBatchNode` that uses as its source texture the same `blank. png` file. Now we are ready to place as many rectangles inside `_gameBatchNode` as we'd like, and set a different color for each one of them if we want. We can, in other words, build an entire test game with one tiny image. Which is what we'll proceed to do now.

4. So to finish up here add these last lines:

```
_terrain = Terrain::create();
_gameBatchNode->addChild(_terrain, kMiddleground);

_player = Player::create();
_gameBatchNode->addChild(_player, kBackground);
```

What just happened?

We just created a placeholder sprite we can use to test gameplay ideas quickly and painlessly. And we created our game's two main objects: the `Player` and `Terrain` objects. These are empty shells at the moment, but we'll start working on them next. But first let's go over the different game elements.

The Player object

This represents our cyclist. It will jump, float, and collide with the `_terrain` object. It's x speed is passed to the _terrain object causing it to move, side scrolling to the left of the screen.

The `Player` object derives, once again, from a `GameSprite` class. This one has getters and setters for next position, vector of movement, and the sprite's width and height.

The `Player` interface has inline helper methods to retrieve information about its rectangle boundaries related to its current position (left, right, top, bottom) and its next position (`next_left`, `next_right`, `next_top`, `next_bottom`). These will be used in collision detection with the `_terrain` object.

The Block object

These objects form the individual pieces of the `_terrain` object. They can take the shape of a building, or an empty gap between buildings. We'll have four different types of buildings, which later will represent four different types of textures when we finally bring in our sprite sheets. These blocks can have different widths and heights.

`Block` also derives from `GameSprite` and it also has inline helper methods to retrieve information about its boundaries, but only in relation to its current position, since `Block` don't technically move.

The Terrain object

This object contains the individual `Block` objects that form the landscape. It contains just enough `Block` objects to fill the screen, and as the `_terrain` object scrolls to the left, the `Block` objects that leave the screen are moved to the far right side of the `_terrain` and reused as new `Blocks`, ensuring continuous scrolling.

The `_terrain` object also is responsible for collision checks with the `_player` object, since it has quick access to all information we'll need for collision detection; namely the list of blocks currently on the screen, their size, type, and position. Our main loop then will call on the `Terrain` object to test for player collision.

Let's work on these main objects, starting with the `Player` object.

Time for action – coding the player

Open up the `Player.cpp` class.

1. `_player` is created through a static method that uses our `blank.png` file to texture the sprite. That method also makes a call to `initPlayer`, and this is what you should type for that method:

```
void Player::initPlayer () {
    this->setAnchorPoint(ccp(0.5f, 1.0f));
    this->setPosition(ccp(_screenSize.width * 0.2f, _
nextPosition.y));

    _height = 228;
    _width = 180;
    this->setTextureRect(CCRectMake(0, 0, _width, _height));
    this->setColor(ccc3(255,255,255));
}
```

The `_player` object will have its registration point at the top of the sprite. The reason behind this top center anchor point has much more to do with the way the `_player`'s object will be animated when floating, than with any collision logic requirements.

2. Next comes `setFloating`:

```
void Player::setFloating (bool value) {

    if (_floating == value) return;

    if (value && _hasFloated) return;

    _floating = value;

    if (value) {
        _hasFloated = true;
        _vector.y += PLAYER_JUMP * 0.5f;
    }
}
```

The `_hasFloated` property will ensure the player can only open the umbrella once while in the air. And when we set `_floating` to `true` we give the `_player` y vector a boost.

3. We begin the `_player`'s update method with:

```
void Player::update (float dt) {
    if (_speed + ACCELERATION <= _maxSpeed) {
        _speed += ACCELERATION;
```

```
    } else {
        _speed = _maxSpeed;
    }

    _vector.x = _speed;
```

The game will increase `_maxSpeed` of the `_player` object as time goes on, making the game more difficult. These first lines make the change from `_players` current `_speed` up to `_maxSpeed` a bit smoother and not an immediate change.

> This game has no levels, so it's important to figure out a way to make it incrementally harder to play, and yet not impossible. Finding that sweet spot in your logic may take some time and it's one more reason to test game ideas as soon as possible. Here we make the game harder by increasing the player's speed and the size of the gaps between buildings. These are updated inside a countdown in the main loop.

4. Next, we update the `_player` object based on its `_state` of movement:

```
switch (_state) {

    case kPlayerMoving:
        _vector.y -= GRAVITY;
        if (_hasFloated) _hasFloated = false;
        break;

    case kPlayerFalling:

        if (_floating ) {
            _vector.y -= FLOATNG_GRAVITY;
            _vector.x *= FLOATING_FRICTION;

        } else {
            _vector.y -= GRAVITY;
            _vector.x *= AIR_FRICTION;
            _floatingTimer = 0;
        }
        break;

    case kPlayerDying:
        _vector.y -= GRAVITY;
        _vector.x = -_speed;
        this->setPositionX(this->getPositionX() + _vector.x);
        break;

}
```

We have different values for gravity and friction depending on move state.

We also have a time limit for how long the _player object can be floating, and we reset that timer when the _player object is not floating. If the _player object is dying (collided with a wall), we move the _player object backwards and downwards until it leaves the screen.

5. We finish with:

```
if (_jumping) {
    _state = kPlayerFalling;
    _vector.y += PLAYER_JUMP * 0.25f;
    if (_vector.y > PLAYER_JUMP ) _jumping = false;
}


if (_vector.y < -TERMINAL_VELOCITY)
    _vector.y = -TERMINAL_VELOCITY;

_nextPosition.y = this->getPositionY() + _vector.y;

if (_floating) {
    _floatingTimer += dt;
    if (_floatingTimer > _floatingTimerMax) {
        _floatingTimer = 0;
        this->setFloating(false);
    }
}
}
```

When the player presses the screen for a jump we shouldn't make the sprite jump immediately. Changes in state should always happen smoothly. So we have a boolean property in _player called _jumping. It is set to true when the player presses the screen and we slowly add the jump force to _vector.y. So the longer the player presses the screen, the higher the jump will be and a quick tap will result in a shorter jump. This is a nice feature to add to any platform game.

We next limit the y speed with a terminal velocity, update the next position of the _player object, and update the floating timer if _player is floating.

What just happened?

The _player is updated through a series of states. Touching the screen will make changes to this _state property, as will the results of collision checking with _terrain.

Now let's work on the Block class.

Time for action – coding the Block object

Once again a static method `create` will use `blank.png` to create our `Block` sprite. Only this time, we don't actually change the texture rectangle for `Block` inside `create`:

1. The `Block` object is properly textured inside the `setupBlock` method:

```
void Block::setupBlock (int width, int height, int type) {

    _type = type;

    _width = width * _tileWidth;
    _height = height * _tileHeight;

    this->setAnchorPoint(ccp(0,0));
    this->setTextureRect(CCRectMake(0, 0, _width, _height));
```

A `Block`'s appearance will be based on its type, width, and height.

The `Block` sprite's registration point is set to top left. And we finally change the `Block`'s texture rectangle size here.

2. Then we set the `Block`'s color based on `type`:

```
switch (type) {

    case kBlockGap:
        this->setVisible(false);
        return;

    case kBlock1:
        this->setColor(ccc3(200,200,200));
        break;

    case kBlock2:
        this->setColor(ccc3(150,150,150));
        break;

    case kBlock3:
        this->setColor(ccc3(100,100,100));
        break;

    case kBlock4:
        this->setColor(ccc3(50,50,50));
```

```
        break;

    }

    this->setVisible(true);

}
```

kBlockGap means there is no building, just a gap the _player object must jump. We make the block invisible in that case and return from the function. So again, gaps are actually types of blocks in our logic.

In this test version the different types of buildings are represented with different colors. Later we'll use different textures.

What just happened?

The Block object is very simple. We just need its values for _width and _height, and whether it's a gap or not so we can properly run collision detection with these objects.

Planning the Terrain class

Before we jump to coding the Terrain class we need to discuss a few things regarding randomness.

It is a very common mistake among game developers to confuse randomness with variableness. It's very important to know which one you need and when.

A random number can be anything. 1234 is a random series of numbers. The next time you want a random series of numbers and you once again get 1234, this will be just as random as the previous one. But not varied.

If you decide to randomly generate terrain you will probably be disappointed in the result as it won't necessarily be varied. Also, remember that we need to make the terrain the key challenge of the game, it can't be too easy or too difficult. True randomness will not allow us enough control here, or worse, we would end up with a long list of conditionals to make sure we have the correct combination of blocks, and that would result in at least one recurrent function inside our main loop that is not a good idea.

We need instead to control the results and their variableness by applying our own patterns to them.

So we'll apply this logic of patterns to our _terrain object, forming a kind of pool of proper *random* choices. We'll use four arrays to store possible results in our decision making, and we'll shuffle three of these arrays during the game to add that "random" feel to our terrain.

The first array is:

```
int patterns[] = {1,1,1,1,2,2,2,2,2,2,2,2,2,2,2,3,3,3};
```

This holds the information of how many buildings (`Blocks`) we have in a row, between gaps.

You can easily change the `patterns` just by adding new values or by increasing or reducing the number of times one value appears. So here we're making a terrain with far more groupings of two buildings between gaps, than groups of three or one.

Next:

```
int widths[] = {2,2,2,2,2,3,3,3,3,3,3,4,4,4,4,4,4};
int heights[] = {0,0,0,0,0,0,0,0,0,0,0,1,1,1,1,1,1,1,2,2,2,3,3,3,3,3,
3,4};
```

The widths and heights of each new building. These will be multiplied with the tile size determined for our game to get the final width and height values, as you saw in `Block:setupBlock`.

We'll use a `0` value for height to mean there is no change in height from the previous building. A similar logic could be easily applied to widths.

And finally:

```
int types[] = {1,2,3,4,1,3,2,4,3,2,1,4,2,3,1,4,2,3,1,2,3,2,3,4,1,2,4,3
,1,3,1,4,2,4,2,1,2,3};
```

These are building types. In play, this array will not be shuffled unlike the three previous ones, so this pattern of types will be used throughout the game and it will loop continuously. You can make it as long as you wish.

Building the Terrain object

Every time we need to create a new block, we'll set it up based on the information contained in these arrays.

This gives us far more control over the terrain, so that we don't create impossible combinations of obstacles for the player: a common mistake in randomly-built terrain for dash games.

Furthermore, we can easily expand this logic to fit every possible need. For instance, we could apply level logic to our game, by creating multiple versions of these arrays, so as the game gets harder, we begin sampling data from arrays that contain particularly hard combinations of values.

And we can still use a conditional loop to refine results even further. I'll give you at least one example of this.

The values you saw in the `patterns` arrays will be stored inside the `vector` lists called: `_blockPattern`, `_blockWidths`, `_blockHeights`, and `_blockTypes`.

The `Terrain` class then takes care of building the game's terrain in three stages. First we initialize the `_terrain` object, creating among other things a pool for `Block` objects. Then we add the first blocks to the `_terrain` object until a minimum width is reached to ensure the whole screen is populated with `Blocks`. And finally we distribute the various objects.

Time for action – initialising our Terrain class

We'll go over these steps next:

1. The first important method to implement is `initTerrain`:

```
void Terrain::initTerrain () {

    _increaseGapInterval = 5000;
    _increaseGapTimer = 0;
    _gapSize = 2;

    _blockPool = CCArray::createWithCapacity(20);
    _blockPool->retain();

    //init object pools
    Block * block;
    for (int i = 0; i < 20; i++) {
        block = Block::create();
        this->addChild(block);
        _blockPool->addObject(block);
    }

    _blocks = CCArray::createWithCapacity(20);
    _blocks->retain();

    _minTerrainWidth = _screenSize.width * 1.5f;

    random_shuffle(_blockPattern.begin(), _blockPattern.end());
    random_shuffle(_blockWidths.begin(), _blockWidths.end());
    random_shuffle(_blockHeights.begin(), _blockHeights.end());

    this->addBlocks(0);
}
```

We have a timer to increase the width of gaps (we begin with gaps two tiles long).

We create a pool for blocks so we don't instantiate any during the game. 20 blocks is more than enough for what we need.

The blocks we are currently using in the terrain will be stored inside a _blocks array.

We determine that the minimum width the _terrain object must have is 1.5 times the screen width. We'll keep adding blocks until the _terrain object reaches this minimum width. We end by shuffling the patterns vectors and adding the blocks.

2. The addBlocks method should look like this:

```
void Terrain::addBlocks(int currentWidth) {

    Block * block;
    while (currentWidth < _minTerrainWidth) {
        block = (Block *) _blockPool-
        >objectAtIndex(_blockPoolIndex);
        _blockPoolIndex++;
        if (_blockPoolIndex == _blockPool->count()) {
            _blockPoolIndex = 0;
        }
        this->initBlock(block);
        currentWidth += block->getWidth();
        _blocks->addObject(block);

    }

    this->distributeBlocks();
}
```

The logic inside the while loop will continue to add blocks until currentWidth of the _terrain object reaches _minTerrainWidth. Every new block we retrieve from the pool in order to reach _minTerrainWidth gets added to _blocks array.

3. Blocks are distributed based on their widths:

```
void Terrain::distributeBlocks() {
    int count = _blocks->count();

    Block * block;
    Block * prev_block;

    for (int i = 0; i < count; i++) {
        block = (Block *) _blocks->objectAtIndex(i);
        if (i != 0) {
            prev_block = (Block *) _blocks->objectAtIndex(i -
            1);
```

```
            block->setPositionX( prev_block->getPositionX() +
            prev_block->getWidth());

        } else {
            block->setPositionX ( 0 );
        }
    }
}
```

What just happened?

`Terrain` is a container of `Blocks`, and we just added the logic that will add a new `block` objects to this container. Inside `addBlocks` we call an `initBlock` method, which will use the information from our `patterns` arrays to initialize each block used in the terrain. It is this method we'll implement next.

Time for action – initializing our Blocks

Finally the method that initializes the blocks based on our `patterns` array.

1. Inside the `Terrain` class, we start the `initBlock` method like this:

    ```
    void Terrain::initBlock(Block * block) {

        int blockWidth;
        int blockHeight;

        int type = _blockTypes[_currentTypeIndex];
        _currentTypeIndex++;

        if (_currentTypeIndex == _blockTypes.size()) {
            _currentTypeIndex = 0;
        }
    ```

    We begin by determining the type of building we are initializing. See how we loop through the `_blockTypes` array using the index stored in `_currentTypeIndex`. We'll use a similar logic for the other `patterns` arrays.

2. Then let's start building our blocks:

    ```
    if (_startTerrain) {
        //...
    } else {
        _lastBlockHeight = 2;
        _lastBlockWidth = rand() % 2 + 2;
        block->setupBlock (_lastBlockWidth, _lastBlockHeight, type);
    }
    ```

The player must tap the screen to begin the game (_startTerrain), until then we show buildings with the same height (two tiles) and random width.

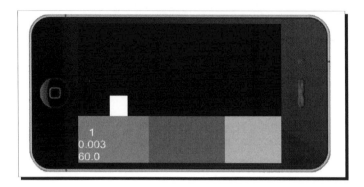

We store _lastBlockHeight and _lastBlockWidth because the more information we have about the terrain, the better we can apply our own conditions to it, as you will see in a moment.

3. If we are set to _startTerrain:

```
if (_startTerrain) {
    if (_showGap) {
        int gap = rand() % _gapSize;
        if (gap < 2) gap = 2;

        block->setupBlock (gap, 0, kBlockGap);
_showGap = false;

    } else {
        //...
```

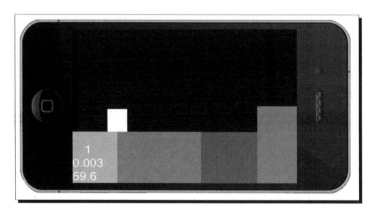

The information inside `_blockPattern` determines how many buildings we show in a row, and once a series is completed we show a gap by setting the `boolean` value of `_showGap` to `true`. A gap's width is based on the current value of `_gapSize`, which may increase as the game gets harder and it can't be less than two times the tile width.

4. If we are not creating a gap this time:

```
} else {

    blockWidth = _blockWidths[_currentWidthIndex];

    _currentWidthIndex++;
    if (_currentWidthIndex == _blockWidths.size()) {
        random_shuffle(_blockWidths.begin(),
        _blockWidths.end());
        _currentWidthIndex = 0;
    }

    if (_blockHeights[_currentHeightIndex] != 0) {

        //change height of next block
        blockHeight = _blockHeights[_currentHeightIndex];
        //if difference too high, decrease it
        if (blockHeight - _lastBlockHeight > 2 && _gapSize ==
        2)
        {
            blockHeight = 1;
        }

    } else {
        blockHeight = _lastBlockHeight;
    }
    _currentHeightIndex++;
    if (_currentHeightIndex == _blockHeights.size()) {
        _currentHeightIndex = 0;
        random_shuffle(_blockHeights.begin(),
        _blockHeights.end());
    }

    block->setupBlock (blockWidth, blockHeight, type);
    _lastBlockWidth = blockWidth;
    _lastBlockHeight = blockHeight;
```

We determine the width and height of the new block based on the current indexed values of `_blockWidths` and `_blockHeights`. Notice how we reshuffle the arrays once we are done iterating through them (`random_shuffle`).

We use `_lastBlockHeight` to apply an extra condition to our terrain. We don't want the next block to be too tall in relation to the previous building, at least not in the beginning of the game. We can determine this by checking the value for `_gapSize`, which is increased as the game gets harder.

And if the value from `_blockHeights` is 0, we don't change the height of the new building and use instead the same value from `_lastBlockHeight`.

5. We finish by updating the count in the current series of buildings, to determine if we should show a gap next, or not:

```
//select next block series pattern
_currentPatternCnt++;

if (_currentPatternCnt > _blockPattern[_currentPatternIndex]) {
    _showGap = true;
    //start new pattern
    _currentPatternIndex++;
    if (_currentPatternIndex == _blockPattern.size()) {
        random_shuffle(_blockPattern.begin(),
        _blockPattern.end());
        _currentPatternIndex = 0;
    }
    _currentPatternCnt = 1;
    }
}
```

What just happened?

We finally got to use our `patterns` arrays and build the blocks inside the terrain. The possibilities are endless here in how much control we have in building our blocks. But the key idea here is to make sure the game does not become ridiculously hard, and I advise you to play some more with the values to achieve even better results (don't take my choices for granted).

Before we tackle collision, let's add the logic to move and reset the terrain.

Time for action – moving and resetting

We move the terrain inside the move method:

1. The method receives as a parameter the amount of movement in the x axis:

```
void Terrain::move (float xMove) {
    if (xMove < 0) return;

    if (_startTerrain) {

        if (xMove > 0 && _gapSize < 5)
            _increaseGapTimer += xMove;

        if (_increaseGapTimer > _increaseGapInterval) {
            _increaseGapTimer = 0;
            _gapSize += 1;
        }
    }

    this->setPositionX(this->getPositionX() - xMove);

    Block * block;
    block = (Block *) _blocks->objectAtIndex(0);

    if (m_tPosition.x + block->getWidth() < 0) {

        _blocks->removeObjectAtIndex(0);
        _blocks->addObject(block);

        m_tPosition.x += block->getWidth();

        float width_cnt = this->getWidth() - block->getWidth()
        - ((Block *) _blocks->objectAtIndex(0))-> getWidth();
        this->initBlock(block);
        this->addBlocks(width_cnt);
    }
}
```

The value for xMove comes from the _player speed.

We start by updating the timer that will make the gaps wider. Then we move the terrain to the left. If after moving the terrain, a block leaves the screen, we move the block back to the end of the _blocks array and reinitialize it as a new block through initBlock.

We make a call to addBlocks just in case the reinitialized block made the total width of the terrain less than the minimum width required.

2. Next, our `reset` method:

```
void Terrain::reset() {

    this->setPosition(ccp(0,0));
    _startTerrain = false;

    int count = _blocks->count();
    Block * block;
    int currentWidth = 0;
    for (int i = 0; i < count; i++) {
        block = (Block *) _blocks->objectAtIndex(i);
        this->initBlock(block);
        currentWidth += block->getWidth();
    }

    while (currentWidth < _minTerrainWidth) {
        block = (Block *) _blockPool-
        >objectAtIndex(_blockPoolIndex);
        _blockPoolIndex++;
        if (_blockPoolIndex == _blockPool->count()) {
            _blockPoolIndex = 0;
        }
        _blocks->addObject(block);
        this->initBlock(block);
        currentWidth += block->getWidth();
    }

    this->distributeBlocks();
    _increaseGapTimer = 0;
    _gapSize = 2;
}
```

The `reset` method is called whenever we restart the game. We move `_terrain` back to its starting point, and we reinitialize all the current `Block` objects currently inside the `_terrain` object. This is done because we are back to `_startTerrain = false`, which means all blocks should have the same height and a random width.

If at the end of the reset we need more blocks to reach `_minTerrainWidth` we add them accordingly.

What just happened?

We can now move the `_terrain` object and all the blocks it contains, and we can restart the process all over if we need to.

Once again using the container behavior of CCNodes simplifies our job tremendously. When you scroll the terrain, you scroll all the Block objects it contains.

So we are finally ready to run collision logic.

Platform collision logic

We have in place all the information we need to check for collision through the inline methods found in Player and Block.

In this game we'll need to check collision between the _player's bottom side and the Block's top side, and between the _player's right side and the Block's left side. We'll do that by checking the _player's current and next position. We are looking for these conditions:

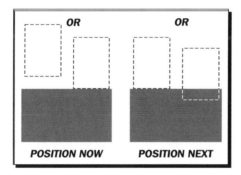

The image represents the conditions for bottom side collision, but the same idea applies to right side collision.

In the current position the _player object must be above the top of the block or touching it. In the next position the _player object must be either touching the top of the block or already overlapping it (or has moved past it altogether). This would mean a collision has occurred.

Time for action – adding collision detection

Let's see how that translates to code:

1. Still in Terrain.cpp:

```
void Terrain::checkCollision (Player * player) {

    if (player->getState() == kPlayerDying) return;
```

```
int count = _blocks->count();
Block * block;
bool inAir = true;

for (int i = 0; i < count; i++) {

    block = (Block *) _blocks->objectAtIndex(i);
    if (block->getType() == kBlockGap) continue;

    //if within x range, check y (bottom collision)
    if (player->right() >= this->getPositionX() + block-
    >left() && player->left() <= this->getPositionX() +
    block->right())
    {

        if (player->bottom() >= block->top() && player-
        >next_bottom() <= block->top() && player->top() >
        block->top())
        {
            player->setNextPosition(ccp(player-
            >getNextPosition().x, block->top() + player-
            >getHeight()));
            player->setVector ( ccp(player->getVector().x,
            0));
            inAir = false;
            break;
        }

    }
}
```

First we state that the _player object is currently falling with inAir = true; we'll let the collision check determine if this will remain true or not.

We don't check for collisions if _player is dying and we skip collision checks with any gap blocks.

We check collision on the y axis, which here means the bottom of the _player and top of the block. We first need to determine if the _player object is within range of the block we want to check against collision. This means the center of the _player object must be between the left and right side of the block. Otherwise the block is too far from the _player object and may be ignored.

Then we run a basic check to see if there is a collision between _player's current position and next position, using the conditions I explained earlier. If so, we fix the _player's position and change its y vector speed to 0 and we determine that inAir = false after all, the _player has landed.

2. Next we check collision on the x axis, meaning the right side of the _player object with the left side of the blocks:

```
for (int i = 0; i < count; i++) {

        block = (Block *) _blocks->objectAtIndex(i);
        if (block->getType() == kBlockGap) continue;

        //now if within y range, check x (side collision)
        if ((player->bottom() < block->top() && player->top() >
        block->bottom()) || (player->next_bottom() < block-
        >top() && player->next_top() > block->bottom()))
        {

                if (player->right() >= this->getPositionX() +
                block->getPositionX() && player->left() < this-
                >getPositionX() + block->getPositionX())
                {

                        player->setPositionX( this->getPositionX() +
                        block->getPositionX() - player->getWidth() *
                        0.5f );
                        player->setNextPosition(ccp(this-
                        >getPositionX() + block->getPositionX() -
                        player->getWidth() * 0.5f, player-
                        >getNextPosition().y));
                        player->setVector ( ccp(player->getVector().x *
                        -0.5f, player->getVector().y) );
                if (player->bottom() + player->getHeight() * 0.2f <
                block->top())
                {
                        player->setState(sprite);
                        return;
                }
                break;
                }
        }
}
```

Similar steps are used to determine if we have a viable block or not.

If we do have a side collision the _player state is changed to kPlayerDying, we reverse its x speed so the _player (state) will move to the left and off the screen, and we return from this method.

3. We end by updating the _player's state based on our collision results:

```
if (inAir) {
    player->setState(kPlayerFalling);
} else {
    player->setState(kPlayerMoving);
    player->setFloating (false);
}
}
```

What just happened?

We just added the collision logic to our platform game. As we've done in our first game, *Air Hockey*, we test the player's current position for collision as well as its next position to determine if a collision occurred between the current iteration and the next one. The test simply looks for overlaps between the player's and block's boundaries.

Adding the controls

It is fairly common in a dash game such as this to have very simple controls. Often the player must only press the screen for jumping. But we spiced things up a bit adding a floating state.

Remember, we want smooth transitions between states, so pay attention to how jumping is implemented: not by immediately applying a force to the player's vector, but by simply changing a boolean property and letting the _player's update method handle the change smoothly.

We'll handle the touch events next.

Time for action – handling touches

Let's go back to GameLayer.cpp and add our game's final touches (pun intended).

1. First we work on our CCTouchesBegan method:

```
void GameLayer::ccTouchesBegan(CCSet* pTouches, CCEvent* event) {

    if (!_running) {

        if (_player->getState() == kPlayerDying) {
            _terrain->reset();
            _player->reset();
            resetGame();
        }
        return;
    }
```

If we are not running the game and the `_player` object died, we reset the game on the next touch.

2. Next, if the terrain has not started:

```
if (!_terrain->getStartTerrain()) {
    _terrain->setStartTerrain ( true );
    return;
}
```

Remember that at first the buildings are all the same height and there are no gaps. Once the player presses the screen, we begin changing that through `setStartTerrain`.

3. We finish with:

```
CCTouch *touch = (CCTouch *)pTouches->anyObject();

if (touch) {

    if (_player->getState() == kPlayerFalling) {
        _player->setFloating ( _player->getFloating() ?
        false : true );
    } else {

        if (_player->getState() != kPlayerDying) _player-
        >setJumping(true);
    }

}
}
```

Now we are in play, and if the `_player` object is falling, we either open or close the umbrella, whichever the case may be, through a call to `setFloating`.

And if the `_player` is not falling, nor dying, we make it jump with `setJumping(true)`.

4. If a touch ends, we just need to stop any jumps:

```
void GameLayer::ccTouchesEnded(CCSet* pTouches, CCEvent* event) {
    _player->setJumping(false);
}
```

What just happened?

We added the logic for the game's controls. The `_player` object will change to floating if currently falling, or to jump if currently riding on top of a building, if a touch is detected.

It's time to add our main game loop.

Time for action – coding the main loop

Finally, the last part in our logic.

1. Inside `GameLayer.cpp`:

```
void GameLayer::update(float dt) {

    if (!_running) return;


    if (_player->getPositionY() < -_player->getHeight() ||
        _player->getPositionX() < -_player->getWidth() * 0.5f)
        {

            _running = false;

        }
}
```

If the `_player` is off screen, we stop the game.

2. Now update all the elements positions and check for collision:

```
_player->update(dt);

    _terrain->move(_player->getVector().x);

    if (_player->getState() != kPlayerDying)
        _terrain->checkCollision(_player);

    _player->place();
```

3. Move `_gameBatchNode` in relation to the `_player` object:

```
if (_player->getNextPosition().y > _screenSize.height * 0.6f) {
        _gameBatchNode->setPositionY( (_screenSize.height *
        0.6f - _player->getNextPosition().y) * 0.8f);

    } else {
        _gameBatchNode->setPositionY ( 0 );
    }
```

4. And make the game more difficult as time goes on by increasing the _player's maximum speed:

```
if (_terrain->getStartTerrain() && _player->getVector().x > 0) {

        _speedIncreaseTimer += dt;
        if (_speedIncreaseTimer > _speedIncreaseInterval) {
            _speedIncreaseTimer = 0;
            _player->setMaxSpeed (_player->getMaxSpeed() + 4);
        }
    }


}
```

What just happened?

We have our test game in place. From here we can test our terrain patterns, our speeds, and our general gameplay to find spots where things could be improved.

We should check in particular if the game gets too hard too fast, or if we have combinations of buildings that are just impossible to get past.

I find, for instance, that starting with larger groups of buildings, say four of five, and then slowly reducing them to two and one between gaps can make the game even more fun to play, so the patterns could be changed to reflect that idea.

Summary

Every game has at its core a simple gameplay idea. But often this idea needs a whole lot of testing and improvement before we can determine if it's fun or not, which is why rapid prototyping is vital.

We can use Cocos2d-x to quickly test core gameplay ideas and run them in the simulator or on a device in a matter of minutes.

Also, the techniques shown here can be used to build interface elements (like the energy bar from our previous game) as well as an entire game! If you don't believe me, check out the game *Square Ball* in an App store near you.

Now with all the gameplay logic in place, we can proceed to making this game look good! We'll do that in the next chapter.

7

Adding the Looks – Victorian Rush Hour

Now that we have our test game, it's time to make it all pretty! We'll go over the new sprite elements added to make the game look nice, and cover a new topic or two. But by now you should be able to understand everything in the final code of this project.

So you can sit back and relax a bit. This time I won't make you type so much. Promise.

In this chapter you will learn:

- ◆ How to use multiple sprites to texture a tiled terrain
- ◆ How to use multiple containers inside a CCSpriteBatchNode
- ◆ How to create a parallax effect
- ◆ How to add a menu to your game
- ◆ How to build a game tutorial

Victorian Rush Hour – the game

Download the file `7341_07_START_PROJECT.zip` from this book's support page (`www.packtpub.com/support`), and run the project in Xcode. You should be able to recognize all the work we did in the test version, and pinpoint the extra elements we added; although nothing was added to the actual gameplay.

In Victorian Rush Hour, I wanted to make the terrain the main challenge in the game, but I also wanted to show you how easily you can add new elements to the buildings and interact with them.

You can later use the same logic to add enemies, obstacles, or pickups for the cyclist sprite. All you need to do is extend the collision detection logic to check on the new items. You could for instance add umbrellas as pickups, and every time the `_player` floated he would be minus one umbrella.

Next, I'll list the new elements added to the game.

New sprites

Quite a few sprites were added to our game:

♦ There is a group of cyclists at the beginning of the game representing the rush traffic.

♦ We add a background layer (cityscape) and a foreground layer (lampposts) to help us with our parallax effect. The clouds in the background are also part of the effect.

♦ We add chimneys to the buildings. These puff smoke as the player taps the screen.

♦ And of course the usual stuff: score label, game logo, and a game over message.

Animations

Some of the sprites now run animation actions:

- The `_player` sprite runs an animation `_rideAnimation`, showing him riding the bicycle.

- Also added was our old friend, the swinging animation, shown when the `_player` is floating (`_floatAnimation`). This is the reason for the odd registration point on the cyclist sprite, as the swing animation looks better if the sprite's anchor point is not centered.

- Our group of cyclists are also animated during the intro section of the game, and are moved offscreen when the game starts (`_jamAnimate`, `_jamMove`).

- We show a puff of smoke coming out of the chimneys whenever the player jumps. This animation is stored inside the new `Block.cpp` class and is created through a series of actions, including a frame animation (`_puffAnimation`, `_puffSpawn`, `_puffMove`, `_puffFade`, and `_puffScale`).

- In `GameLayer.cpp`, when the `_player` dies, we run a few actions on a `_hat` sprite to make it rise in the air and drop down again, just to add some humor.

Now let's go over the added logic.

Texturing our buildings with CCSprites

In the test version we just coded, our game screen was divided into tiles of 128 pixels in the iPad retina screen. The width and height properties of the `Block` objects are based on this measurement. So a building two tiles wide, and three tiles tall would have in effect 256 pixels in width and 384 pixels in height. A gap too would be measured this way, though its height is set to 0.

The logic we use to texture the buildings will take these tiles into account.

So let's take a look at the code to add texture to our buildings.

Time for action – texturing the buildings

Perform the following steps to texture buildings:

1. Each `Block` will store references to four different types of texture representing the four types of buildings used in the game (`_tile1`, `_tile2`, `_tile3`, and `_tile4`). So in the `initBlock` method we now store that information:

```
void Block::initBlock() {

    _tile1 = CCSpriteFrameCache::sharedSpriteFrameCache()
    ->spriteFrameByName ("building_1.png");
    _tile2 = CCSpriteFrameCache::sharedSpriteFrameCache()
    ->spriteFrameByName ("building_2.png");
    _tile3 = CCSpriteFrameCache::sharedSpriteFrameCache()
    ->spriteFrameByName ("building_3.png");
    _tile4 = CCSpriteFrameCache::sharedSpriteFrameCache()
    ->spriteFrameByName ("building_4.png");
```

2. Each `Block` also stores references to two types of texture for the building roof tile (`_roof1` and `_roof2`):

```
    _roof1 = CCSpriteFrameCache::sharedSpriteFrameCache()
      ->spriteFrameByName ("roof_1.png");
    _roof2 = CCSpriteFrameCache::sharedSpriteFrameCache()
      ->spriteFrameByName ("roof_2.png");
```

3. Next we create and distribute the various `CCSprite` tiles that form our building:

```
//create tiles
int i;
_wallTiles = CCArray::createWithCapacity(20);
_wallTiles->retain();

_roofTiles = CCArray::createWithCapacity(5);
_roofTiles->retain();

CCSprite * tile;

//place CCSprite tiles (each building has 5 columns and 4
//rows)
for (i = 0; i < 5; i++) {
  tile = CCSprite::createWithSpriteFrameName("roof_1.png");
  tile->setAnchorPoint(ccp(0, 1));
  tile->setPosition(ccp(i * _tileWidth, 0));
  tile->setVisible(false);
  this->addChild(tile, kMiddleground, kRoofTile);
```

```
_roofTiles->addObject(tile);

for (int j = 0; j < 4; j++) {
    tile = CCSprite::createWithSpriteFrameName
    ("building_1.png");
    tile->setAnchorPoint(ccp(0, 1));
    tile->setPosition(ccp(i * _tileWidth, -1 *
    (_tileHeight * 0.47f + j * _tileHeight)));
    tile->setVisible(false);
    this->addChild(tile, kBackground, kWallTile);
    _wallTiles->addObject(tile);
}

}
```

A Block is comprised of 20 CCSprites stored inside a _wallTiles array and five CCSprites stored in a _roofTiles array. So when we initialize a Block object, we in effect create a building that is five tiles wide and four tiles tall. I made the decision that no building in the game would exceed this size. If you decide to change this, then here is where you will make your changes.

4. The initBlock method also creates five chimney sprites and places them at the top of the building. These will be spread out later according to the building type and could be very easily turned into obstacles for our _player. We also create the animation actions for the puffs of smoke, here inside initBlock.

5. Moving on to our new setupBlock method, this is where the unnecessary tiles and chimneys are turned invisible and where we spread out the visible chimneys. We begin the method as follows:

```
void Block::setupBlock (int width, int height, int type) {

    this->setPuffing(false);

    _type = type;

    _width = width * _tileWidth;
    //add the roof height to the final height of the block
    _height = height * _tileHeight + _tileHeight * 0.49f;
    this->setPositionY(_height);

    CCSpriteFrame * wallFrame;
    CCSpriteFrame * roofFrame = rand() % 10 > 6 ? _roof1 :
    _roof2;

    int num_chimneys;
    float chimneyX[] = {0,0,0,0,0};
```

6. Then based on building type, we give different x positions for the chimney sprites and determine the texture we'll use on the wall tiles.

```
switch (type) {

    case kBlockGap:
        this->setVisible(false);
        return;

    case kBlock1:
        wallFrame = _tile1;
        chimneyX[0] = 0.2f;
        chimneyX[1] = 0.8f;
        num_chimneys = 2;
        break;
    case kBlock2:
        wallFrame = _tile2;
        chimneyX[0] = 0.2f;
        chimneyX[1] = 0.8f;
        chimneyX[2] = 0.5f;
        num_chimneys = 3;
        break;
    case kBlock3:
        wallFrame = _tile3;
        chimneyX[0] = 0.2f;
        chimneyX[1] = 0.8f;
        chimneyX[2] = 0.5f;
        num_chimneys = 3;

        break;
    case kBlock4:
        wallFrame = _tile4;
        chimneyX[0] = 0.2f;
        chimneyX[1] = 0.5f;
        num_chimneys = 2;
        break;
}
```

7. The method then proceeds to position the visible chimneys. We finally move to texturing the building. The logic to texture the roof and wall tiles is the same; for instance, here's how the walls are tiled by changing the texture of each `CCSprite` wall through the `setDisplayFrame` method, and then turning unused tiles invisible:

```
count = _wallTiles->count();
    for (i  = 0; i < count; i++) {
        tile = (CCSprite *) _wallTiles->objectAtIndex(i);
```

```
        if (tile->getPositionX() < _width && tile
      ->getPositionY() > -_height) {
        tile->setVisible(true);
        tile->setDisplayFrame(wallFrame);
      } else {
        tile->setVisible(false);
      }
    }
  }

}
```

What just happened?

When we instantiate a `Block` in `initBlock`, we create a 5 x 4 building made out of wall tiles and roof tiles, each a `CCSprite`. And when we need to turn this building into a 3 x 2 building, or 4 x 4 building, or whatever, we simply turn the excess tiles invisible at the end of `setupBlock`.

The texture used for the roof is picked randomly, but the one picked for the walls is based on building type (from our pattern array). It is also inside this `for` loop that all the tiles positioned at a point greater than the new building's width and height are turned invisible.

Containers within containers

Before we move to the parallax effect logic, there is something I wanted to talk about related to the layering of our `_gameBatchNode`, which you'll recall is a `CCSpriteBatchNode` object.

If you go to the static `create` method inside `Terrain.cpp`, you will notice that the object is still created with a reference to a `blank.png` texture:

```
terrain->initWithSpriteFrameName("blank.png")
```

In fact the same 1x1 pixel image used in the test version is now in our sprite sheet, only this time the image is transparent.

This is a bit of a hack, but necessary, because a sprite can only be placed inside a batch node if its texture source is the same used to create the batch node. Now `Terrain` is just a container, it has no texture. But by setting its "blank" texture to something contained in our sprite sheet, we can place `_terrain` inside `_gameBatchNode`.

The same thing is done with the `Block` class, which now, in the final version of the game, behaves as another textureless container. It will contain the various `CCSprites` for the wall and roof tiles as well as chimneys and puff animations as its children.

The organization of the layers inside our _gameBatchNode object can seem complex and at times even absurd. After all in the same node we have a foreground "layer" of lampposts, a middle-ground "layer" of buildings, and a background "layer" containing a cityscape. The player is also placed in the background but on top of the cityscape. And not only that but all three layers are moved at different speeds to create our parallax effect, and all this inside the same CCSpriteBatchNode!

But the amount of code this arrangement saves us justifies any confusion we might have at times keeping the batch node organized. Now we can animate the puffs of smoke, for instance, and never worry about keeping them "attached" to their respective chimney sprite as the terrain scrolls to the left. The container will take care of keeping things together.

Creating a parallax effect

Cocos2d-x has a special CCNode called CCParallaxNode, and one surprising thing about it is how little you get to use it! CCParallaxNode helps create parallax effect with finite layers, or finite scrolling, meaning you can use it if your game screen has a limit to how much it can scroll each way. Implementing CCParallaxNode to a game screen that can scroll indefinitely, such as the one in Victorian Rush Hour, usually requires more effort than it takes to build your own effect.

A parallax effect is created by moving objects at different depths by different speeds. The farther a layer appears from the screen, the slower its speed should be. In a game this usually means that the player sprite's speed is fractioned and sent to all the layers that appear behind it, and multiplied for the layers that appear in front of the player sprite.

Let's add this to our game.

Time for action – creating a parallax effect

Perform the following steps to create a parallax effect:

1. The parallax effect in our game takes place inside the main loop in the following lines of code:

```
//update parallax
if (_player->getVector().x > 0) {
  _background->setPositionX(_background->getPosition().x -
  _player->getVector().x * 0.25f);
```

First we move the `_background` sprite, which contains the cityscape texture repeated three times along the x axis, and we move it at one fourth the speed of the `_player` sprite.

2. The `_background` scrolls to the left, and as soon as the first cityscape texture is off the screen, we shift the entire `_background` container to the right at precisely the spot where the second cityscape texture would appear if allowed to continue. We get this value by subtracting where the sprite would be from the total width of the sprite:

```
float diffx;

if (_background->getPositionX() < -_background
  ->getContentSize().width) {
  diffx = fabs(_background->getPositionX()) - _background
  ->getContentSize().width;
  _background->setPositionX(-diffx);
}
```

So in effect we only ever scroll the first texture sprite inside the container.

3. A similar process is repeated with the `_foreground` sprite and the three lamppost sprites it contains, only the `_foreground` moves at four times the speed of the `_player` sprite:

```
_foreground->setPositionX(_foreground->getPosition().x - _player-
>getVector().x * 4);

if (_foreground->getPositionX() < -_foreground
  ->getContentSize().width * 4) {
  diffx = fabs(_foreground->getPositionX()) - _foreground
  ->getContentSize().width * 4;
  _foreground->setPositionX(-diffx);
}
```

4. And we also employ our cloud sprites in the parallax effect. Since they appear behind the cityscape, so even farther away from the _player, the clouds move at an even lower rate (0.15):

```
int count = _clouds->count();
CCSprite * cloud;
for (int i = 0; i < count; i++) {
   cloud = (CCSprite *) _clouds->objectAtIndex(i);
   cloud->setPositionX(cloud->getPositionX() - _player
   ->getVector().x * 0.15f);
   if (cloud->getPositionX() + cloud
   ->boundingBox().size.width * 0.5f < 0 )
   cloud->setPositionX(_screenSize.width + cloud
   ->boundingBox().size.width * 0.5f);
   }
}
```

What just happened?

We just added the parallax effect in our game by simply using the player speed at different ratios at different depths. The only slightly complicated part of the logic is how to ensure the sprites scroll continuously. But the math of it is very simple. You just need to make sure the sprites align correctly.

Adding a menu to our game

Right now we only see the game logo on our intro screen. We need to add buttons to start the game and also for the option of playing a tutorial.

In order to do that, we'll use a special kind of CCLayer, which is the CCMenu.

CCMenu is a collection of CCMenuItemSprites. The layer is responsible for distributing its items as well as tracking touch events on all items.

Time for action – creating CCMenu and CCMenuItem

Perform the following steps to create CCMenu and CCMenuItem:

1. In `GameLayer.cpp`, scroll down to the `createGameScreen` method. We'll add the new logic to the end of this method.

2. First, create the menu item for our start game button:
```
CCSprite * menuItemOn;
CCSprite * menuItemOff;

menuItemOn = CCSprite::createWithSpriteFrameName ("btn_new_
on.png");
menuItemOff = CCSprite::createWithSpriteFrameName ("btn_new_off.
png");

CCMenuItemSprite * starGametItem = CCMenuItemSprite::create (
  menuItemOff,
  menuItemOn,
  this,
  menu_selector (GameLayer::startGame)
);
```

We create a `CCMenuItemSprite` object by passing it one sprite per state of the button. When the user touches a `CCMenuItemSprite`, the off state sprite is turned invisible and the on state sprite is turned visible, all inside the touch began event. On touch ended or touch cancelled, the off state is displayed once again.

We also pass the callback function for this item, in this case `GameLayer::StartGame`.

3. Next we add the tutorial button:
```
menuItemOn = CCSprite::createWithSpriteFrameName
  ("btn_howto_on.png");


menuItemOff = CCSprite::createWithSpriteFrameName
  ("btn_howto_off.png");

CCMenuItemSprite * howToItem = CCMenuItemSprite::create (
  menuItemOff,
  menuItemOn,
  this,
  menu_selector (GameLayer::showTutorial));
```

4. Then it's time to create the menu:

```
_mainMenu = CCMenu::create(howToItem, starGametItem, NULL);

_mainMenu->alignItemsHorizontallyWithPadding(120);
_mainMenu->setPosition(ccp(_screenSize.width * 0.5f,
  _screenSize.height * 0.54));

this->addChild(_mainMenu, kForeground);
```

The `CCMenu` constructor can receive as many `CCMenuItemSprites` as you wish to display. These items are then distributed with one of the following calls: `alignItemsHorizontally`, `alignItemsHorizontallyWithPadding`, `alignItemsVertically`, `alignItemsVerticallyWithPadding`, `alignItemsInColumns`, and `alignItemsInRows`. The items items appear in the order they are passed to the `CCMenu` constructor.

5. Then we need to add our call back functions:

```
void GameLayer::startGame (CCObject* pSender) {
  _tutorialLabel->setVisible(false);
  _intro->setVisible(false);
  _mainMenu->setVisible(false);

  _jam->runAction(_jamMove);
  SimpleAudioEngine::sharedEngine()
  ->playEffect("start.wav");
  _terrain->setStartTerrain ( true );
  _state = kGamePlay;
}

void GameLayer::showTutorial (CCObject* pSender) {
  _tutorialLabel->setString
  ("Tap the screen to make the player jump.");
  _state = kGameTutorialJump;
  _jam->runAction(_jamMove);
  _intro->setVisible(false);
  _mainMenu->setVisible(false);
  SimpleAudioEngine::sharedEngine()
  ->playEffect("start.wav");
  _tutorialLabel->setVisible(true);

}
```

These are called when our menu buttons are pressed, one method to start the game, and one to show the tutorial.

What just happened?

We just created our game's main menu. CCMenu can save us a lot of time handling all the interactivity logic of buttons. Though it might not be as flexible as other items in Cocos2d-x, it's good to know it's there if we need it.

We'll tackle the tutorial section next.

Adding a tutorial to our game

Let's face it. With the possible exception of Air Hockey, every game so far in this book could benefit from a tutorial, or a "how to play" section. With Victorian Rush Hour, I'm going to show you a quick way to implement one.

The unspoken rule of game tutorials is: make it playable. And that's what we'll attempt to do here.

We'll create a game state for our tutorial, and we'll add a CCLabelTTF object to our stage, and make it invisible unless the tutorial state is on. We'll use the CCLabelTTF to display our tutorial text.

Let us go over the steps necessary to create our game tutorial.

Time for action – adding a tutorial

Perform the following steps to add a tutorial:

1. Back to the `createGameScreen` method, add the following lines to create our `CCLabelTTF` object:

```
_tutorialLabel = CCLabelTTF::create
    ("", "Times New Roman", 80);
_tutorialLabel->setPosition(ccp
    (_screenSize.width * 0.5f, _screenSize.height * 0.6f) );

this->addChild(_tutorialLabel, kForeground);
_tutorialLabel->setVisible(false);
```

2. We add four states to our enumerated list of game states. These will represent the different steps in our tutorial:

```
typedef enum {
    kGameIntro,
    kGamePlay,
    kGameOver,
    kGameTutorial,
    kGameTutorialJump,
    kGameTutorialFloat,
    kGameTutorialDrop

} GameState;
```

The first tutorial state, `kGameTutorial`, acts as a separator from all other game states. So if the value for `_state` is greater than `kGameTutorial`, we are in tutorial mode.

Depending on the mode, we display a different message and we wait on a different condition to change to a new tutorial state.

3. If you recall, our `showTutorial` method starts with a message telling the player to tap the screen to make the sprite jump:

```
_tutorialLabel->setString
    ("Tap the screen to make the player jump.");
_state = kGameTutorialJump;
```

4. Then in the `update` method, at the end of the method, we start adding the lines that will display the rest of our tutorial information. First if the player sprite is in the midst of a jump and has just begun falling:

```
if (_state > kGameTutorial) {
    if (_state == kGameTutorialJump) {
```

```
if (_player->getState() == kPlayerFalling && _player
->getVector().y < 0) {
  _player->stopAllActions();
  _jam->setVisible(false);
  _jam->stopAllActions();
  _running = false;
  _tutorialLabel->setString
  ("While in the air, tap the screen to float.");
  _state = kGameTutorialFloat;
}
```

As you can see, we let the player know that another tap will open the umbrella and cause the sprite to float.

5. Next as the sprite is floating, when it reaches a certain distance from the buildings, we inform the player that another tap will close the umbrella and cause the sprite to drop:

```
} else if (_state == kGameTutorialFloat) {
  if (_player->getPositionY() < _screenSize.height *
  0.95f) {
    _player->stopAllActions();
    _running = false;
    _tutorialLabel->setString
    ("While floating, tap the screen again to drop.");
    _state = kGameTutorialDrop;
  }
```

6. After that the tutorial is completed, and we show the message that the player may start the game:

```
} else {
  _tutorialLabel->setString
  ("That's it. Tap the screen to play.");
  _state = kGameTutorial;
}
}
```

Whenever we change a tutorial state, we pause the game momentarily and wait for a tap. We handle the rest of our logic inside ccTouchesBegan, so we'll add that next.

7. Inside ccTouchesBegan, in the switch statement, add the following cases:

```
case kGameTutorial:
  _tutorialLabel->setString("");
  _tutorialLabel->setVisible(false);
  _terrain->setStartTerrain ( true );
```

```
    _state = kGamePlay;
    break;

case kGameTutorialJump:
  if (_player->getState() == kPlayerMoving) {
    SimpleAudioEngine::sharedEngine()
    ->playEffect("jump.wav");
    _player->setJumping(true);
  }
  break;

case kGameTutorialFloat:
  if (!_player->getFloating()) {
    _player->setFloating (true);
    _running = true;
  }
  break;

case kGameTutorialDrop:
  _player->setFloating (false);
  _running = true;
  break;
```

What just happened?

We added a tutorial to our game! As you can see we used quite a few new states. But now we can incorporate the tutorial right into our game, and have one flow smoothly into the other. All these changes can be seen in action in the final version of this project, `7341_07_FINAL_PROJECT.zip`, which you can find at this book's support page.

Summary

Having got all our gameplay details ironed out in our test game, bringing in a sprite sheet and game states seems remarkably simple and easy.

But during this stage we can also think of new ways to improve gameplay. For instance, the realization that clouds of smoke coming out of chimneys would offer a nice visual cue to the player to identify where the buildings were, if the cyclist happened to jump too high. Or that a hat flying through the air could be funny!

Now it's time to bring physics to our games, so head on to the next chapter.

8
Getting Physical – Box2D

It's time to tackle physics! Cocos2d-x comes bundled with templates for projects utilizing either Box2D or Chipmunk. These are so-called 2D physics engines; the first written in C++ and the second in C. Chipmunk has a more recent Objective-C port but Cocos2d-x must use the original one written in C for portability.

We'll be using Box2D for the examples in this book. The last two games I'll show you will be developed with that engine, starting with a simple pool game to illustrate all the main points about using Box2D in your projects.

What you will learn:

- ◆ How to create a project that incorporates Box2D
- ◆ How to set up and run a Box2D simulation
- ◆ How to create bodies
- ◆ How to use the debug draw feature to quickly test your concepts
- ◆ How to use collision filters and listeners

Creating a Box2D project with Cocos2d-x

Let's start by going over the various steps involved in creating a Box2D project with Cocos2d-x. We begin by firing up Xcode and choosing **File** | **New** | **Project**.

This time, we select the **cocos2dx_box2d** template option.

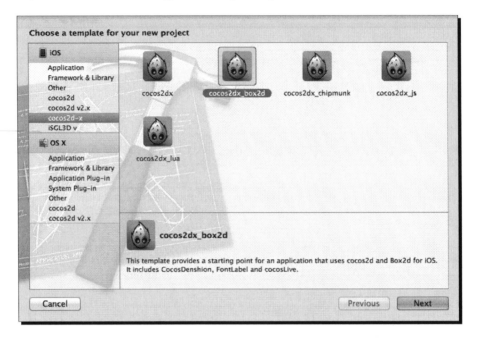

Name your project whatever you want, and save it. The template will create a `HelloWorld` project that includes in its libraries the source code for Box2D.

If you run the project as-is in your iPhone simulator, you should see something like this:

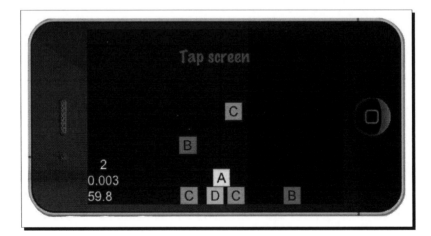

Now it's time to do some cleaning.

Time for action – preparing the basic template

Please understand that the following steps are all optional. I happen not to like the way the Box2D project template is set up:

1. Go to the folder where you extracted the framework and locate the `Test` files, this time go to `samples/TestCpp/Classes/Box2DTestBed`.

2. Drag the `GLES-Render.h` and `GLES-Render.cpp` files from `Box2DTestBed` to your project `Classes` group. Make sure to select **Copy items into destination...** and make sure you selected your project as the target.

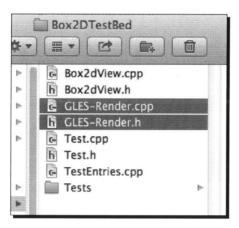

3. In the `HelloWorldScene.h` header file, leave the includes in place, but change the class declarations to match this much shorter one:

```
class HelloWorld : public cocos2d::CCLayer {
public:
    ~HelloWorld();
    HelloWorld();

    // returns a Scene that contains the HelloWorld class as the
only child
    static cocos2d::CCScene* scene();

    void initPhysics();
    virtual void draw();
    void update(float dt);

private:
    b2World* world;
};
```

4. Then add this include:

```
#include "GLES-Render.h"
```

5. And add this private member:

```
GLESDebugDraw * m_debugDraw;
```

6. Then in the `HelloWorldScene.cpp` implementation file replace the lines between `using namespace CocosDenshion` and the `HelloWorld::scene` method with these:

```
#define PTM_RATIO 32

HelloWorld::HelloWorld()
{
    this->initPhysics();
    scheduleUpdate();
}

HelloWorld::~HelloWorld()
{
    delete world;
    world = NULL;

    delete m_debugDraw;
}

void HelloWorld::initPhysics() {

    b2Vec2 gravity;
    gravity.Set(0.0f, -10.0f);
    world = new b2World(gravity);

    // Do we want to let bodies sleep?
    world->SetAllowSleeping(true);
    world->SetContinuousPhysics(true);

    m_debugDraw = new GLESDebugDraw( PTM_RATIO );
    world->SetDebugDraw(m_debugDraw);

    uint32 flags = 0;
    flags += b2Draw::e_shapeBit;
    //      flags += b2Draw::e_jointBit;
    //      flags += b2Draw::e_aabbBit;
    //      flags += b2Draw::e_pairBit;
```

```
//          flags += b2Draw::e_centerOfMassBit;
m_debugDraw->SetFlags(flags);

}

void HelloWorld::draw()
{
    //
    // IMPORTANT:
    // This is only for debug purposes
    // It is recommend to disable it
    CCLayer::draw();

    ccGLEnableVertexAttribs( kCCVertexAttribFlag_Position );

    kmGLPushMatrix();

    world->DrawDebugData();

    kmGLPopMatrix();
}

void HelloWorld::update(float dt)
{
    world->Step(dt, 8, 1);

}
```

What just happened?

The GLES-Render class is necessary to use the debug draw feature in Box2D. This will draw all the elements from the simulation on the screen. The debug draw object is created inside the initPhysics method alongside the Box2D simulation (b2World). We'll go over that logic in a moment.

As the comment inside the draw method states, the debug draw feature should be switched off once you're done developing your game. So, all the lines pertaining to that object, as well as the draw method, should be commented out.

So what is a physics engine?

The famous Isaac Newton said: every action has a reaction. Right after he said *who the hell threw that apple?*

So far in our games we have covered very simple collision systems, basically only ever checking to see if simple shapes (circles and rectangles) overlapped each other. The reaction from these collisions also were very simple in our games so far, using vector inversions or simply by making things disappear once they touch. With Box2D you get much more!

Box2D is a very robust collision detection engine and can certainly be used just for that purpose. But the simulation will also process and return a bunch of information derived from the collisions and the interactions between bodies, including how the objects should behave, based on their shapes, mass, and all the forces at play in the simulation.

Meet Box2D

At the core of the engine you have the b2World object. This is the simulation. You fill the world with b2Body objects, and then you step through the simulation with b2World->Step(). You take the results of the simulation and display them to the user through your sprites, by grabbing a b2Body's position and rotation and applying them to a sprite.

The debug draw object allows you to see the simulation without using any sprites. A way to quickly test and prototype your game, like we did in *Chapter 6, Quick & Easy Sprite: Victorian Rush Hour*.

Meet the world

Most of the time, the physics simulation will require the creation of a b2world object. However, you can get interesting results by managing more than one world object in the same game, for multiple views for instance. But that's for another book.

In our simplified basic project, the world is created like this:

```
b2Vec2 gravity;
gravity.Set(0.0f, -10.0f);
world = new b2World(gravity);

// Do we want to let bodies sleep?
world->SetAllowSleeping(true);
world->SetContinuousPhysics(true);

m_debugDraw = new GLESDebugDraw( PTM_RATIO );
world->SetDebugDraw(m_debugDraw);

uint32 flags = 0;
flags += b2Draw::e_shapeBit;
//          flags += b2Draw::e_jointBit;
//          flags += b2Draw::e_aabbBit;
//          flags += b2Draw::e_pairBit;
//          flags += b2Draw::e_centerOfMassBit;
m_debugDraw->SetFlags(flags);
```

Box2D has its own vector structure, `b2Vec2`, and we use it here to create the world's gravity. The `b2World` object receives that as its parameter. A simulation does not always require gravity of course; in that case the argument will be a `(0, 0)` vector.

`SetAllowSleeping` means that if objects are not moving and are therefore not generating derived data, skip checking for derived data from those objects.

`SetContinuousPhysics` means we have some fast objects in our hands, which we'll later point out to the simulation, so it can pay extra attention for collisions.

Then we create the debug draw object. This is optional, as I said before. The flags indicate what you wish to see in the drawing. In the previous code we only want to see the shapes of the objects.

Then comes `PTM_RATIO`, the defined constant that we passed as a parameter to the debug draw. Box2D uses meters instead of pixels for a variety of reasons that are, entirely unnecessary for anyone to know. But keep this one thing in mind: every pixel position value used in the game will be divided by this ratio constant (PTM stands for pixel to meter). If the result from this division ever gets above 10 or below 0.1, increase or decrease the value for `PTM_RATIO` accordingly.

Though you have some leeway, of course. By all means, play with this value once your game is completed, and pay special attention to the subtle differences in speed (another common value for this ratio is 100).

Running the simulation

As I said before you use the step method to run the simulation, usually inside your main loop, though not necessarily.

```
world->Step(dt, 8, 1);
```

You need to pass it the time step, here represented by the delta time in the main loop, and then pass it the number of velocity iterations and position iterations in the step. This basically means how many times, inside a step, velocity and position will be processed.

In the previous example, I'm using the default values from the Box2D template in Cocos2d-x. Usually a fixed time step is better than the delta, and a higher value for the position iteration may be necessary if things move really fast in your game. But remember always to play with these values, aiming at finding the lowest possible ones.

No CCObjects in Box2D

So, no memory management. So please remember to get rid of all of the Box2D objects through `delete` and not `release`. If you `new` it... well, you remember:

```
HelloWorld::~HelloWorld(){
    delete world;
    world = NULL;

    delete m_debugDraw;
}
```

Meet the bodies

The `b2Body` object is the thing you'll spend most of your time dealing with inside a Box2D simulation. You have three main types of `b2Bodies`: dynamic, static, and kinematic. The first two are of greater importance, and are the ones we'll use in our game.

Bodies are created by combining a body definition with a body fixture. The body definition is a structure that holds information about type, position, velocity, and angle, among other things. The fixture holds information about the shape, including its density, elasticity, and friction.

So to create a circle that is, 40 pixels wide, you would use the following code:

```
b2BodyDef bodyDef;
bodyDef.type = b2_dynamicBody;
//or make it static bodyDef.type = b2_staticBody;
b2Body * body = world->CreateBody(&bodyDef);

//create circle shape
b2CircleShape  circle;
circle.m_radius = 20.0/PTM_RATIO;

//define fixture
b2FixtureDef fixtureDef;
fixtureDef.shape = &circle;
fixtureDef.density = 1;
fixtureDef.restitution = 0.7;
fixtureDef.friction = 0.4;

body->CreateFixture(&fixtureDef);
```

To create a box that is 40 pixels wide you would use the following code:

```
//create body
b2BodyDef bodyDef;
bodyDef.type = b2_dynamicBody;
```

```
b2Body * body = world->CreateBody(&bodyDef);

//define shape
b2PolygonShape box;
box.SetAsBox(20 /PTM_RATIO, 20 / PTM_RATIO);

//Define fixture
b2FixtureDef fixtureDef;
fixtureDef.shape = &box;
fixtureDef.density = 2;
fixtureDef.restitution = 0;
body->CreateFixture(&fixtureDef);
```

Notice that you use the `world` object to create the bodies. And also notice that boxes are created at half their desired width and height.

Density, friction, and restitution all have default values so you don't always need to set these.

Our game – MiniPool

Our game consists of sixteen balls (circles), one cue (box), and a pool table made out of six lines (edges) and six pockets (circles).

Download the final project from this book's support page if you wish to follow along with the final code. Box2D is a complex API and it will be best to review and expose the logic rather than work on it by doing a lot of typing. So there will be no start project to work from this time.

Game settings

This is a portrait-only, with no screen rotation allowed, universal application. The game is designed for the regular iPhone (320 x 480) and its resolution size is set to `kResolutionShowAll`. This will show borders around the main screen in devices that do not match the 1.5 screen ratio of the iPhone:

```cpp
//in AppDelegate.cpp
CCSize designSize = CCSize(320, 480);

CCEGLView::sharedOpenGLView()->setDesignResolutionSize(designSize.
width, designSize.height, kResolutionShowAll);

if (screenSize.width > 640) {
    CCFileUtils::sharedFileUtils()->setResourceDirectory("ipadhd");
    pDirector->setContentScaleFactor(1280/designSize.width);
} else if (screenSize.width > 320) {
    CCFileUtils::sharedFileUtils()->setResourceDirectory("ipad");
    pDirector->setContentScaleFactor(640/designSize.width);
} else {
    CCFileUtils::sharedFileUtils()->setResourceDirectory("iphone");
    pDirector->setContentScaleFactor(320/designSize.width);
}
```

Notice that I use the iPhone's dimensions to identify larger screens. So the iPad and iPhone retina are considered to be two times 320 x 480 and the retina iPad is considered to be four times 320 x 480.

CCSprite + b2Body = b2Sprite

The most common way to work with `b2Bodies` in Cocos2d-x is to combine them with `CCSprites`. In the games I'll show you, I created a class called `b2Sprite` that extends `CCSprite` with the addition of a `_body` member property that points to its very own `b2Body`. I also add a few helper methods to deal with our pesky `PTM_RATIO`, and please feel free to add as many of these as you think necessary.

`b2Bodies` has an incredibly helpful property called `userData`. You can store anything you wish inside it and the bodies will carry it with them throughout the simulation. So what most developers do is store inside the body's `userData` property a reference to the instance of `CCSprite` that is wrapping it. So `b2Sprite` knows about its body, and the body knows about its `b2Sprite`.

 As a matter of fact, composition is key when working with Box2D. So when designing your games make sure that every object knows of every other object or can get to them quickly. This will help immensely.

Creating the pool table

In the debug draw view this is what the table looks like:

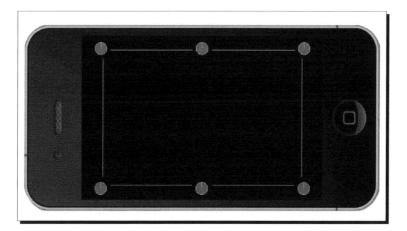

All of the elements seen here are created inside the `initPhysics` method in `GameLayer. cpp`. The table has no visual representation other than the background image that we use in the game. So there is no sprite attached to the individual pockets, for example.

The `pocket` bodies are created inside a `for` loop, with the best algorithm I could come up with to distribute them correctly on screen. This logic is found in the `initPhysics` method, so let's take a look at that and see how our first `b2Bodies` are created:

```
b2Body * pocket;
b2Sprite * pocketData;
b2CircleShape circle;
float startX = _screenSize.width * 0.07;
float startY = _screenSize.height * 0.92f;
for (int i = 0; i < 6; i++) {
    bodyDef.type = b2_staticBody;
    if (i < 3) {
        bodyDef.position.Set(startX/PTM_RATIO,
(startY - i * (_screenSize.height * 0.84f * 0.5f))/PTM_RATIO);

    } else {
        bodyDef.position.Set(
        (startX + _screenSize.width * 0.85f)/PTM_RATIO,
        (startY - (i-3) * (_screenSize.height * 0.84f *
        0.5f))/PTM_RATIO);
    }
    pocket = _world->CreateBody(&bodyDef);
    fixtureDef.isSensor = true;
```

```
circle.m_radius = (float) (1.5 * BALL_RADIUS) / PTM_RATIO;
fixtureDef.shape = &circle;

pocket->CreateFixture(&fixtureDef);
pocketData = new b2Sprite(this, kSpritePocket);
pocket->SetUserData(pocketData);
}
```

The `pockets` bodies are static bodies and we determine in their fixture definition that they should behave as sensors:

```
fixtureDef.isSensor = true;
```

This switches off all of the physics from an object and turns it into a collision hot spot. A sensor serves only to determine if something is touching it or not.

>
> It's almost always best to ignore Box2D sensors and use your own sprites or `CCPoints` in your collision logic. One neat feature with sensors is that they make it very easy to determine when something has just ceased touching them, as you'll see once we cover contact listeners.

Creating edges

If a shape can only be hit on one side, an edge is probably what you need. Here is how we create edges in our game:

```
b2BodyDef tableBodyDef;
tableBodyDef.position.Set(0, 0);
b2Body* tableBody = _world->CreateBody(&tableBodyDef);

// Define the table edges
b2EdgeShape tableBox;

// bottom edge
tableBox.Set(b2Vec2(_screenSize.width * 0.14f/PTM_RATIO, _screenSize.
height * 0.09f/PTM_RATIO),
b2Vec2(_screenSize.width * 0.86f/PTM_RATIO, _screenSize.height *
0.09f/PTM_RATIO));
tableBody->CreateFixture(&tableBox,0);

// top edge
tableBox.Set(b2Vec2(_screenSize.width * 0.14f/PTM_RATIO, _screenSize.
height * 0.91f/PTM_RATIO),
    b2Vec2(_screenSize.width * 0.86f/PTM_RATIO, _screenSize.height *
0.91f/PTM_RATIO));
tableBody->CreateFixture(&tableBox,0);
```

So the same `b2Body` object can have as many edges as you need. You `Set` an edge with its start and end points (in this case, the `b2Vec2` structures) and add it as a fixture to the body, with a 0 density.

Creating the ball objects

In the game there is a class called `Ball` that extends `b2Sprite`, used for both the target balls and the cue ball. These objects are also created inside the `initPhysics` method. Here is the basic configuration for that object:

```
//create Box2D body
b2BodyDef bodyDef;
bodyDef.type = b2_dynamicBody;

_body = _game->getWorld()->CreateBody(&bodyDef);
_body->SetLinearDamping(1.2f);
_body->SetAngularDamping(0.2f);

//create circle shape
b2CircleShape  circle;
circle.m_radius = BALL_RADIUS/PTM_RATIO;

//define fixture
b2FixtureDef fixtureDef;
fixtureDef.shape = &circle;
fixtureDef.density = 5;
fixtureDef.restitution = 0.7f;

//add collision filters so only white ball can be hit by cue
if (_type == kSpriteBall) {
    fixtureDef.filter.categoryBits = 0x0010;
} else if (_type == kSpritePlayer) {
//white ball is tracked as bullet by simulation
    _body->SetBullet(true);
    fixtureDef.filter.categoryBits = 0x0100;
}

//set sprite texture
switch (_color) {
    case kColorBlack:
        this->initWithSpriteFrameName("ball_black.png");
        break;
    case kColorRed:
        this->initWithSpriteFrameName("ball_red.png");
```

```
            break;
        case kColorYellow:
            this->initWithSpriteFrameName("ball_yellow.png");
            break;
        case kColorWhite:
            this->initWithSpriteFrameName("ball_white.png");
            break;
    }

    _body->CreateFixture(&fixtureDef);
    //store the b2Sprite as the body's userData
    _body->SetUserData(this);
```

The `friction` fixture property involves the reaction of two touching surfaces (two bodies). In this case we want to create "friction" with the table surface, which is not a body at all. So what we need to use instead is damping. This will apply a similar effect to friction but without the need of an extra surface. Damping can be applied to the linear velocity vector of a body:

```
    _body->SetLinearDamping(1.2);
```

And to the angular velocity:

```
    _body->SetAngularDamping(0.2);
```

Also, the white ball is set to be a bullet:

```
    _body->SetBullet(true);
```

This will make the simulation pay extra attention to this object in terms of collision. We could make all balls in the game behave as bullets, but this is not only unnecessary (something revealed through testing) but also not very processing-friendly.

Creating collision filters

In the `ball` object there is a `filter` property inside the fixture definition that we use to mask collisions. This means that, we determine what bodies can collide with each other. The cue ball receives a different value for `categoryBits` than the other balls:

```
    fixtureDef.filter.categoryBits = 0x0100;
```

When we create the cue body we set a `maskBits` property in its fixture definition:

```
    fixtureDef.filter.maskBits = 0x0100;
```

We set this to the same value as the white ball, `categoryBits`.

What is the result of all this? Now the cue can only hit bodies with the same `categoryBits`, which here means the cue can only collide with the white ball.

It is possible to add more than one category to a mask by using the | option

```
fixtureDef.filter.maskBits = 0x0100 | 0x0010;
```

Or to collide with everything except the cue ball, for instance:

```
fixtureDef.filter.maskBits = 0xFFFF & ~0x0100;
```

Creating the cue ball

The cue ball also extends `b2Sprite` and its body is set as a box.

```
//create body
b2BodyDef bodyDef;
bodyDef.type = b2_dynamicBody;

_body = _game->getWorld()->CreateBody(&bodyDef);
_body->SetLinearDamping(8);
_body->SetAngularDamping(5);

//Define shape
b2PolygonShape box;
box.SetAsBox(BALL_RADIUS * 21 /PTM_RATIO, BALL_RADIUS * 0.2 /
PTM_RATIO);

//Define fixture
b2FixtureDef fixtureDef;
fixtureDef.shape = &box;
fixtureDef.filter.maskBits = 0x0100;
fixtureDef.density = 10;
fixtureDef.restitution = 1;
_body->CreateFixture(&fixtureDef);
_body->SetUserData(this);
```

It has very high damping values because in the rare occasions when the player misses the cue ball, the cue will not fly off the screen but halt a few pixels from the white ball.

If we wanted to create the cue ball as a trapezium or a triangle, we would need to give the `b2PolygonShape` property, the vertices we want:

```
b2Vec2 vertices[3];
vertices[0].Set(0.0f, 0.0f);
vertices[1].Set(1.0f, 0.0f);
```

```
vertices[2].Set(0.0f, 1.0f);
int32 count = 3;

b2PolygonShape triangle;
triangle.Set(vertices, count);
```

The vertices must be added counter-clockwise to the array. This means that if we add the top vertex of the triangle first, the next vertex must be the one to the left.

Once all elements are in place the debug draw looks like this:

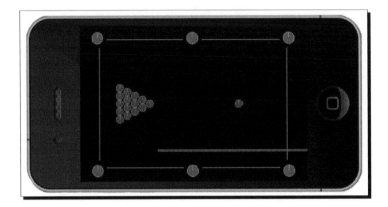

Creating a contact listener

In addition to collision filters, one other feature in Box2D that helps with collision management is the creation of a contact listener.

Inside the `initPhysics` method we create the world object like this:

```
b2Vec2 gravity;
gravity.Set(0.0f, 0.0f);
_world = new b2World(gravity);

_world->SetAllowSleeping(true);
_world->SetContinuousPhysics(true);
_collisionListener = new CollisionListener();
_world->SetContactListener(_collisionListener);
```

Our `CollisionListener` class extends the Box2D `b2ContactListener` class, and it must implement at least one of the following methods:

```
void BeginContact(b2Contact* contact);
void EndContact(b2Contact* contact);
void PreSolve(b2Contact* contact, const b2Manifold* oldManifold);
void PostSolve(b2Contact* contact, const b2ContactImpulse* impulse);
```

These events are all related to a contact (collision) and are fired at different stages of
a contact.

 Sensor objects can only ever fire the `BeginContact` and
`EndContact` events.

In our game we implement two of these methods. The first is:

```
void CollisionListener::BeginContact(b2Contact* contact) {
    b2Body * bodyA = contact->GetFixtureA()->GetBody();
    b2Body * bodyB = contact->GetFixtureB()->GetBody();

    b2Sprite * spriteA = (b2Sprite *) bodyA->GetUserData();
    b2Sprite * spriteB = (b2Sprite *) bodyB->GetUserData();

    if (spriteA && spriteB) {
        //track collision between balls and pockets
        if (spriteA->getType() == kSpritePocket) {
            spriteB->setVisible(false);
        } else if (spriteB->getType() == kSpritePocket) {
            spriteA->setVisible(false);
        } else if (spriteA->getType() == kSpriteBall &&
            spriteB->getType() == kSpriteBall) {
            if (spriteA->mag() > 10 || spriteB->mag() > 10) {
            SimpleAudioEngine::sharedEngine()->
            playEffect("ball.wav");
            }
        } else if ((spriteA->getType() == kSpriteBall &&
                    spriteB->getType() == kSpritePlayer) ||
                   (spriteB->getType() == kSpriteBall &&
                    spriteA->getType() == kSpritePlayer)) {
            if (spriteA->mag() > 10 || spriteB->mag() > 10) {
                SimpleAudioEngine::sharedEngine()->
                playEffect("ball.wav");
            }
        }
    }
}
```

You can see now how important the `userData` property is. We can quickly access
`CCSprites` attached to the bodies listed in the `b2Contact` object through the
`userData` property.

Besides that, all our sprites have a `_type` property which behaves as an identifying tag in our logic. You could certainly use the Cocos2d-x tags for that, but I find that at times if you can combine the `CCSprite` tags with their `_type` value you may produce interesting sorting logic.

So in `BeginContact` we track collisions between balls and pockets. But we also track collisions between balls. In the first case, the balls are turned invisible when they touch the pockets. And in the second case we play a sound effect whenever two balls touch each other, but only if they are at a certain speed (we determine that through a `b2Sprite` helper method that retrieves the squared magnitude of a sprite's velocity vector).

The other method in our listener is:

```
void CollisionListener::PreSolve(b2Contact* contact, const b2Manifold*
oldManifold)  {

    b2Body * bodyA = contact->GetFixtureA()->GetBody();
    b2Body * bodyB = contact->GetFixtureB()->GetBody();

    b2Sprite * spriteA = (b2Sprite *) bodyA->GetUserData();
    b2Sprite * spriteB = (b2Sprite *) bodyB->GetUserData();


    if (spriteA && spriteB) {

    //track collision between player and cue ball
        if (spriteA->getType() == kSpriteCue && spriteA->mag() > 2) {
            if (spriteB->getType() == kSpritePlayer && spriteA->
            isVisible()) {
                SimpleAudioEngine::sharedEngine()->
                playEffect("hit.wav");
                spriteA->setVisible(false);
                spriteB->getGame()->setCanShoot(false);
            }
        } else if (spriteB->getType() == kSpriteCue && spriteA->mag()
        > 2) {
            if (spriteA->getType() == kSpritePlayer && spriteB->
            isVisible()) {
                SimpleAudioEngine::sharedEngine()->
                playEffect("hit.wav");
                spriteB->setVisible(false);
                spriteA->getGame()->setCanShoot(false);
            }
        }

    }
}
```

Here, we listen to a collision before the reactions are calculated. If there is a collision between the cue and white ball we play a sound effect and we hide the cue.

 If you want to force your own logic for collision reactions and override Box2D on this you should do so in the `PreSolve` method. In this game, however, we could have added all of this collision logic to the `BeginContact` method and it would work just as well.

The game controls

In the game the player must press on the white ball and then drag his or her finger to activate the cue body. The farther the finger gets from the white ball the more powerful the shot will be.

So let's add the events to handle user input.

Time for action – adding the touch events

We'll deal with `CCTouchesBegan` first.

1. In the `ccTouchesBegan` method we start by updating the game state:

```
void GameLayer::ccTouchesBegan(CCSet* touches, CCEvent* event) {

    if (!_running) return;

    if (_gameState == kGameOver) {
        if (_gameOver->isVisible()) _gameOver->setVisible(false);
        resetGame();
        return;
    }
```

2. Next we check on the value of `_canShoot`. This returns `true` if the white ball is not moving:

```
    if (!_canShoot) return;
```

3. Next we determine if the touch is landing on the white ball. If it is, we start the game, if it is not currently running, and we make our timer visible:

```
CCTouch *touch = (CCTouch *)touches->anyObject();

if (touch) {

    CCPoint tap = touch->getLocation();
    CCPoint playerPos = _player->getPosition();
```

```
        float diffx = tap.x - playerPos.x;
        float diffy = tap.y - playerPos.y;
        float diff = pow(diffx, 2) + pow(diffy, 2);
        if (diff < pow(BALL_RADIUS * 4, 2)) {
            if (_gameState != kGamePlay) {
                _gameState = kGamePlay;
                if (_intro->isVisible()) _intro->setVisible(false);
                _timer->setVisible(true);
            }
        }
    }
}
```

Notice that we use a larger radius for the white ball in our logic (four times larger). This is because we don't want the target area to be too small, since this game will run on both iPhones and iPads. We want the player to be able to comfortably hit the white ball with his or her finger.

4. We store where on the ball the touch lies. In this way the player can hit the ball at different points, causing it to move in different angles:

```
//make point lie within ball
if (diff > pow(BALL_RADIUS * 2, 2)) {
    float angle = atan2(diffy, diffx);
    _cueStartPoint = ccp(
            playerPos.x + BALL_RADIUS * 0.8f * cos(angle),
            playerPos.y + BALL_RADIUS * 0.8f * sin(angle));
} else {
    _cueStartPoint = playerPos;
}
```

Because we made the white ball a much larger target for our touch event, now we must make sure that the actual point picked by the player lies within the ball. So we may have to make some adjustments here.

5. We pass the point to our LineContainer object and we prepare the cue body to be used:

```
_lineContainer->setBallPoint(_cueStartPoint);
_cue->getBody()->SetLinearVelocity(b2Vec2(0,0));
_cue->getBody()->SetAngularVelocity(0.0);
_touch = touch;
```

We once again have a LineContainer node, so we can draw a dashed line between the cue and the spot on the ball where the cue will hit. This serves as a visual aid for the player to prepare his or her shot.

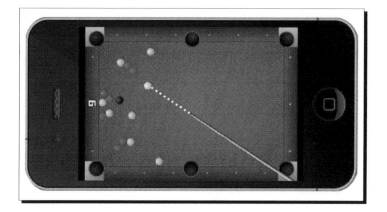

6. In ccTouchesMoved we only need to move the cue body based on the position of the player's finger. So we calculate the distance between the moving touch and the white ball. If the cue body is still too close to the ball we set its body to sleep and its texture invisible:

```
void GameLayer::ccTouchesMoved(CCSet* touches, CCEvent* event) {
    //check for a valid touch first

    CCPoint tap = touch->getLocation();
    float diffx = tap.x - _player->getPositionX();
    float diffy = tap.y - _player->getPositionY();
    if (pow(diffx,2) + pow(diffy,2) < pow(BALL_RADIUS * 2,2)) {
        _usingCue = false;
        _lineContainer->setDrawing(false);
        _cue->setVisible(false);
        _cue->getBody()->SetAwake(false);
    } else {
        _usingCue = true;
        _cue->setVisible(true);
        _lineContainer->setDrawing(true);
        placeCue(tap);
        _cue->getBody()->SetAwake(true);
    }
}
```

7. Otherwise, we awake the body and call the placeCue method:

```
void GameLayer::placeCue(CCPoint position) {
    float diffx = _cueStartPoint.x - position.x;
    float diffy = _cueStartPoint.y - position.y;

    float angle = atan2(diffy, diffx);
```

```
float distance = sqrt(pow (diffx, 2) + pow(diffy, 2));

_pullBack = distance * 0.5f;
CCPoint cuePosition = ccp(
    _cueStartPoint.x - (BALL_RADIUS * 21 + _pullBack) *
    cos(angle),
    _cueStartPoint.y - (BALL_RADIUS * 21 + _pullBack) *
    sin(angle)
);

_cue->getBody()->SetTransform(
    b2Vec2(cuePosition.x/PTM_RATIO,
    cuePosition.y/PTM_RATIO),
    angle);

_lineContainer->setCuePoint(ccp(
    _cueStartPoint.x - ( _pullBack) * cos(angle),
    _cueStartPoint.y - ( _pullBack) * sin(angle)));
}
```

This method then calculates the angle and position of the cue body, and transforms the cue's b2Body method accordingly. The b2Body's SetTransform method takes care of both its position and angle.

8. Finally, in ccTouchesEnded, we let go of the cue body:

```
void GameLayer::ccTouchesEnded(CCSet* touches, CCEvent* event) {

    if (_usingCue && _touch) {
        b2Body * cueBody = _cue->getBody();
        float angle = cueBody->GetAngle();

        //release cue!
        cueBody->ApplyLinearImpulse(
            b2Vec2 (_pullBack * cos(angle) * SHOT_POWER,
            _pullBack * sin(angle) * SHOT_POWER),
            cueBody->GetWorldCenter());
    }

    _usingCue = false;
    _touch = NULL;
    _lineContainer->setDrawing(false);
}
```

We use `ApplyLinearImpulse`. This method receives a vector for the impulse to be applied and the position on the body at which this impulse should be applied.

The `_pullback` variable stores the information of how far the cue body was from the ball when the player released the cue body. The farther it was, the stronger the shot will be.

What just happened?

We added the `touch` events that allow the player to hit the white ball with the cue body. The process is a very simple one. We first need to make sure that the player is touching the white ball, and then we move the cue body as the player drags his or her finger. Finally, when the touch is released, we make the cue spring towards the white ball by using `ApplyLinearImpulse`.

We may also move a body in Box2D by using `SetLinearVelocity` or `ApplyForce`, each with subtle and not so subtle differences and I recommend that you play around with these.

The main loop

As I showed you before, the simulation only requires that you call its `Step()` method inside the main loop. Box2D takes care of all the calculations.

What remains is the rest of the game logic: scoring, game states, and updating your sprites to match the `b2Bodies` method.

It's important to call the `update` method of each ball and cue. This is what our `b2Sprite` update method looks like:

```
void b2Sprite::update(float dt) {
    if (_body && this->isVisible()) {
        this->setPositionX(_body->GetPosition().x * PTM_RATIO);
        this->setPositionY(_body->GetPosition().y * PTM_RATIO);
        this->setRotation(CC_RADIANS_TO_DEGREES(-1 * _body-
>GetAngle()));
    }
}
```

All you need to do is make sure that the `CCSprite` method matches the information in the `b2Body` object. Also, make sure that you convert meters back to pixels when you do so.

So let's add our main loop.

Time for action – adding the main loop

Inside our main loop, we update our b2World object:

1. Start by updating the simulation:

```
void GameLayer::update(float dt) {

    if (!_running) return;
    if (_gameState == kGameOver) return;
    _world->Step(dt, 10, 10);
```

2. Next, we need to determine if the game has finished, by checking on the number of balls currently in play:

```
//track invisible objects
int count = _balls->count();
Ball * ball;

for (int i = 0; i < count; i++) {

    ball = (Ball *) _balls->objectAtIndex(i);

    if (!ball->isVisible() && ball->getInPlay()) {
        ball->setInPlay(false);
        ball->hide();
        //count down balls
        _ballsInPlay--;
        SimpleAudioEngine::sharedEngine()->
        playEffect("drop.wav");
        if (_ballsInPlay == 0) {
            _gameState = kGameOver;
            _gameOver->setVisible(true);
        }
    } else {
        ball->update(dt);
    }
}
```

3. Next we continue to update the sprites:

```
if (!_cue->isVisible())  {
    _cue->hide();
} else {
    _cue->update(dt);
}
```

```
if (!_player->isVisible()) {
    _player->reset();
    _player->setVisible(true);
    SimpleAudioEngine::sharedEngine()-
    >playEffect("whitedrop.wav");
}
_player->update(dt);
```

4. And we also determine when it's time to allow the player to take a new shot. I decided to only let that happen if the white ball has stopped. And the quickest way to determine that is to check on its vector:

```
//check to see if player ball is slow enough for a new shot
if (_player->mag() < 0.5f && !_canShoot) {
    _player->getBody()->SetLinearVelocity(b2Vec2_zero);
    _player->getBody()->SetAngularVelocity(0);
    _canShoot = true;
}
```

What just happened?

We added our main loop. This will update the Box2D simulation, and then it's up to us to take care of positioning our sprites based on the resulting information.

One very important aspect of Box2D is to understand what can be changed inside a b2World::Step call and what can't.

For instance, a body cannot be made inactive (b2Body::SetActive) or be destroyed (b2World::DestroyBody) inside a step. You will need to check on conditions outside the step in order to make these changes. For instance, in our game we check to see if the ball sprites are visible or not, and if not then we set their bodies as inactive. And all this logic takes place after b2World::Step.

Adding a timer to our game

In MiniPool we count the number of seconds it takes the player to clear the table. Let me show you how to do that.

Time for action – creating a timer

We create timers in pretty much the same way as we create our main loop.

1. First, we add a second scheduled event by adding this line to our GameLayer constructor:

```
this->schedule(schedule_selector(GameLayer::ticktock), 1.5f);
```

2. With this, we create a separate timer that will run the `ticktock` method every 1.5 seconds (I decided in the end that 1.5 seconds looked better).

3. The method keeps updating the value of the `_time` property and displaying it in the `_timer` label:

```
void GameLayer::ticktock() {
    if (_gameState == kGamePlay) {
        _time++;
        CCString * value = CCString::createWithFormat("%i", _
time);
        _timer->setString(value->getCString());
    }
}
```

What just happened?

We added a timer to our game by scheduling a second update, specifying the time interval we wanted, using the `schedule` method.

If you wish to remove a timer, all you need to do is call the `unschedule(SEL_SCHEDULE selector)` method of `CCNodes`, anywhere in your class.

Have a go hero

A few changes to make gameplay more interesting could be: add a limit to the number of times the white ball can hit a pocket. Another option is to have the timer work as a countdown, so the player has a limited time to clear the table before time runs out.

Also, this game could do with a few animations. A `CCAction` method to scale down and fade out a ball when it hits a pocket would look very nice.

Pop quiz

Q 1. What is the main object in a Box2D simulation?

1. `b2Universe`
2. `b2d`
3. `b2World`
4. `b2Simulation`

Q 2. A b2Body object can be of type:

1. b2_dynamicBody, b2_sensorBody, b2_liquidBody
2. b2_dynamicBody, b2_staticBody, b2_kinematicBody
3. b2_staticBody, b2_kinematicBody, b2_debugBody
4. b2_kinematicBody, b2_transparentBody, b2_floatingBody

Q 3. Which properties can be set in a fixture definition?

1. density, friction, restitution, shape
2. position, density, bullet state
3. angular damping, active state, friction
4. linear damping, restitution, fixed rotation

Q 4. If two bodies have the same unique value for their maskBits property in their fixture definition, this means:

1. The two bodies can never collide.
2. The two bodies will only trigger begin contact events.
3. The two bodies can only collide with each other.
4. The two bodies will only trigger end contact events.

Summary

Nowadays it seems that everybody in the world has played or will play a physics-based game at some point in their lives. Box2D is by far the most popular engine in the casual games arena. The commands you learned here can be found in pretty much every port of the engine, including a JavaScript one that is growing in popularity by the day.

Setting up the engine and getting it up and running is remarkably simple. Perhaps too much so. A lot of testing and value tweaking goes into developing a Box2D game, and pretty soon you learn that keeping the engine performing as you wish is the most important skill to master when developing physics-based games. Picking the right values for friction, density, restitution, damping, time step, PTM ratio, and so on, can make or break your game.

In the next chapter, we'll continue to use Box2D, but we'll focus on what else Cocos2d-x can do to help us organize our games.

9
The Last Game – Eskimo

In our last game, we'll go over some important features required by most games, but which are not directly related to gameplay. So we'll step over the architecture side of things and talk about reading and writing data, using scene transitions, and creating custom events that your whole application may listen to.

But, of course, I'll add a few gameplay ideas as well!

This time you'll learn how to:

- Create CCScene transitions
- Load external data
- Save data using UserDefault
- Create your own game events with notifications
- Use the accelerometer
- Reuse Box2D bodies

The game – Eskimo

Little eskimo boy is late for supper. It is your mission, should you choose to accept it, to guide the little fella back to his igloo.

This is a Box2D game, and the controls are very simple: Tilt the device and the eskimo will move. If you tap the screen the eskimo switches shape between a snow ball and a block of ice, each shape with its own physical characteristics and degrees of maneuverability. The ball is subject to friction, for instance, whereas the block of ice has none.

And the only way the eskimo may reach his destination is by hitting the gravity switches spread out all over the screen.

Eskimo then combines elements from an arcade game with elements of a puzzle game, as each level was planned with one perfect solution in mind, as to how to take the little eskimo home. Although multiple solutions are possible.

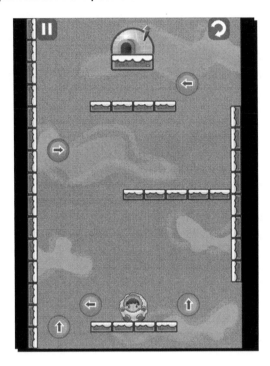

Please download the 7341_09_FINAL_PROJECT.zip and run the game when you have a chance. Once again there is no need for extraneous typing as the logic used in the game is pretty much old news to you; we'll go over the new bits in depth.

The game settings

This is a portrait-only game and uses the accelerometer, so it should not auto-rotate. It is designed for the regular iPhone and its screen resolution size set to kResolutionShowAll. So the screens settings are similar to the ones in our previous game.

Designing a game for the iPhone screen and using the kResolutionShowAll parameter will result in the so called "letterbox" view when playing the game in screens that do not match the iPhone's 1.5:1 ratio. This means you see borders around the game screen. Alternatively you could use the kResolutionNoBorders parameter, which results in a "zoom in" effect causing the game to play at full screen but the areas around the borders will be cropped.

The following image illustrates these two cases:

The one on the left is the game screen on the iPad, using kResolutionShowAll. The one on the right uses kResolutionNoBorders. Notice on the second one how the screen is zoomed in and cropped. When using kResolutionNoBorders it's important to design your game so that no vital gameplay element appears too close to the borders, as it may not be displayed.

How the game is organized

Once again there is a b2Sprite class, and the Eskimo and Platform classes extend b2Sprite. Then there are regular CCSprite classes, GSwitch (that stands for gravity switch) and Igloo. The logic runs collision detection between these last two and Eskimo, but I chose not to have them as sensor bodies because I wanted to show you that 2D collision logic for the Cocos2d-x elements can coexist with collision logic for the Box2D elements just fine.

But most importantly this game now has three CCScenes. So far in this book we've only used one scene per game. This game's scene objects will wrap: MenuLayer, LevelSelectLayer, and GameLayer.

In MenuLayer you have the option to play the game, which will take you to LevelSelectLayer or to play a tutorial for the game, which will take you to GameLayer with no level selected.

In LevelSelectLayer you may choose which available level you want to play, and that will take you to GameLayer. Or you may go back to MenuLayer.

In GameLayer you play the game, and may go back to MenuLayer upon game over.

The following image illustrates all three scenes in the game:

Using CCScenes in Cocos2d-x

CCScenes are mini applications themselves. If you have experience as an Android developer you may think of CCScenes as **Activities**. Of all the CCNode based classes, the CCScene application is the most architecturally relevant, because the CCDirector class runs a CCScene object, in effect running your application.

Part of the good in working with scenes is also part of the bad: they are wholly independent and ignorant of each other. The need to share information between CCScenes will be a major factor when planning your game class structure.

Also, memory management may become an issue. A currently running CCScene will not give up its ghost until a new scene is up and running. So, when you use transition animations, keep in mind that both scenes will need to exist in memory for a few seconds.

In Eskimo I initialize scenes in two different ways. With MenuLayer and LevelSelectLayer, each time the user navigates to either one of these scenes, a new layer object is created (either new MenuLayer or new LevelSelectLayer).

But GameLayer is different. It is a singleton CCLayer class that never stays out of memory after its first instantiation. This may not work for every game, however. As I mentioned earlier, when transitioning between scenes, both scenes stay in memory for a few seconds. But here we are adding to that problem, by keeping one layer in memory the whole time. Eskimo, however, does not take up a lot of memory. We could still create special conditions for when GameLayer should be destroyed, and conditions when it should not create, if we wish.

So let me show you how to create scene transitions. First, a CCScene class that creates a fresh copy of its CCLayer each time it's created.

Time for action – creating a CCScene transition

You have of course been using CCScenes all along:

1. Hidden in AppDelegate.cpp you've had lines like:

```
CCScene *pScene = GameLayer::scene();
// run
pDirector->runWithScene(pScene);
```

2. So in order to change scenes all you need to do is tell the Director which scene you wish to run. Cocos2d-x then will get rid of all the content in the current scene, if any (all their destructors will be called), and then a new layer will be instantiated and wrapped inside new CCScene.

3. Breaking the steps down a little further, this is how you usually create a new scene for CCDirector:

```
CCScene* MenuLayer::scene()
{
    // 'scene' is an autorelease object
    CCScene *scene = CCScene::create();

    // add layer as a child to scene
    CCLayer* layer = new MenuLayer();
    scene->addChild(layer);
    layer->release();

    return scene;
}
```

4. The static MenuLayer::scene method will create a blank scene, then create a new instance of MenuLayer and add it as a child to the new scene.

5. Now you can tell the director to run it:

```
CCDirector::sharedDirector()->replaceScene(MenuLayer::scene());
```

6. The logic changes a little if you wish to use a transition effect. So inside our MenuLayer.cpp this is how we transition to LevelSelectLayer:

```
CCScene* newScene = CCTransitionMoveInR::create(0.2f,
LevelSelectLayer::scene());
CCDirector::sharedDirector()->replaceScene(newScene);
```

The code just described creates a new transition object, which will slide in the new scene from the right side of the screen, to lay on top of the current one. The transition will take 0.2 seconds.

What just happened?

You created a scene transition animation with Cocos2d-x.

As I mentioned earlier, this form of scene change will cause a new instance of the new layer to be created each time, and destroyed each time it's replaced by a new scene. So in our game, `MenuLayer` and `LevelSelectLayer` are instantiated and destroyed as many times as the user switches between them.

There is the option also of using `pushScene` instead of `replaceScene`. This creates a stack of scene objects and keeps them all in memory. This stack can be navigated with `popScene` and `popToRootScene`.

Now let me show you how to do the same thing but with a singleton layer.

 It should be no surprise to you by now that you will find many examples of these transition classes in the `Test` project `samples/TestCPP/Classes/TransitionsTest`.

Time for action – creating transitions with a singleton CCLayer

We first need to make sure the layer in question can only be instantiated once.

1. The `scene` static method in `GameLayer` looks like this:

```
CCScene* GameLayer::scene(int level, int levelsCompleted)
{
    // 'scene' is an autorelease object
    CCScene *scene = CCScene::create();

    // add layer as a child to scene
    scene->addChild(GameLayer::create(level, levelsCompleted));

    return scene;
}
```

This layer receives two parameters when created. The game level it should load and the number of levels completed by the player. We create a new `CCScene` object and add `GameLayer` as its child.

2. But take a look at the static `create` method in `GameLayer`:

```
GameLayer * GameLayer::create (int level, int levelsCompleted) {
    if (!_instance) {
        _instance = new GameLayer();
    } else {
        _instance->clearLayer();
    }
    _instance->setLevelsCompleted(levelsCompleted);
    _instance->loadLevel(level);
    _instance->scheduleUpdate();
    return _instance;
}
```

3. An `_instance` static property is declared at the top of `GameLayer.cpp`:

```
static GameLayer* _instance = NULL;
```

We can check then if the one instance of `GameLayer` is currently in memory, and instantiate it if necessary.

4. The scene transition to `GameLayer` will look, on the surface, to be exactly like the regular kind of transition. So in `LevelSelectLayer` we have:

```
CCScene* newScene = CCTransitionMoveInR::create(0.2f,
GameLayer::scene(_firstIndex + i, _levelsCompleted));
CCDirector::sharedDirector()->replaceScene(newScene);
```

What just happened?

Now we created a `CCScene` transition with a `CCLayer` class that never gets destroyed, so we don't have to instantiate new platform and gravity switch sprites with each new level.

There are of course problems and limitations with this process. We cannot transition between two `GameLayer` objects, for instance, as we only ever have one of them.

There are also some special considerations when leaving `GameLayer` and when getting back to it. For instance, we must make sure we have our main loop running when we get back to `GameLayer`.

The only way to do that is by unscheduling it whenever leaving `GameLayer` and scheduling it again when returning:

```
//when leaving
unscheduleUpdate();
CCScene* newScene = CCTransitionMoveInL::create(0.2f,
MenuLayer::scene());
```

```
CCDirector::sharedDirector()->replaceScene(newScene);

//when returning
_instance->scheduleUpdate();
```

 Again, architecturally speaking there are even better options. Possibly the best one is creating your own game elements cache, or game manager, with object pools, and everything that needs instantiating, stored inside it. And then have this cache be a singleton that every scene can access. This is also the best way to share game relevant data between CCScenes.

Loading external data from a .plist file

Eskimo has only five game levels (feel free to add more), plus a tutorial level. The data for these levels exist inside a `levels.plist` file stored inside the `Resources` folder. A `.plist` file is an XML formatted data file, and as such can be created in any text editor. Xcode, however, offers a nice GUI to edit the files.

Let me show you how to create them inside Xcode.

Time for action – creating a .plist file

You could of course create this in any text editor, but Xcode makes it extra easy to create and edit `.plist` files.

1. Inside Xcode, choose **New | File...** then select `Resource` and `Property List`. When asked where to save the file, choose any location you want:

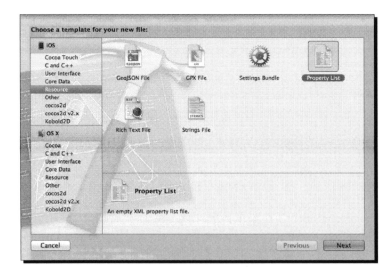

2. You need to decide what the `Root` element of your `.plist` file will be; either an `Array` or a `Dictionary` (the default) type. For Eskimo, the `Root` element is an Array containing a series of Dictionaries, each holding the data for a level in the game.

3. By selecting the `Root` element you get a plus sign indicator right next to the **Type** declaration. Clicking on this plus sign will add an element to `Root`. You may then pick the data type for this new item. The options are: `Boolean`, `Data`, `Date`, `Number`, `String`, and again `Array` and `Dictionary`. The last two can contain sub-items in the tree just like the `Root` element.

4. Keep adding elements to the tree trying to match the items in the following image:

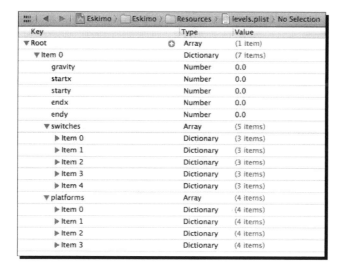

What just happened?

You just created a `Property List` file in Xcode. These are XML structured data that Cocos2d-x can load and parse. You've used them already when loading particles and sprite sheet information.

Loading the level data

In Eskimo, since I only have five levels, I chose to have one `.plist` file containing all levels. This may not be the best option in a larger game.

Although Apple devices will load and parse the `.plist` files quickly, the same may not be true for other targets. So limit the size of your `.plist` files by organizing the data into multiple files. You've probably seen games that divide their levels into multiple groups or packs. This is a simple way to create an extra pre-loading screen that your game can use to parse level data, as well as a means to keep file sizes manageable.

In Eskimo we could have each `.plist` file contain 10 levels for instance, and then 10 `.plist` files, totaling 100 levels.

Time for action – retrieving data from the .plist file

The level data is loaded in GameLayer.

1. Inside the loadLevel method we load the data like this:

```
std::string levelsFile = CCFileUtils::sharedFileUtils()-
>fullPathFromRelativePath("levels.plist");
_levels = CCArray::createWithContentsOfFileThreadSafe(levelsFile
.c_str());
_levels->retain();
```

Cocos2d-x will take care of mapping CCFileUtils to the correct target. There is a CCFileUtils for each platform supported by the framework, and they can all be made to work with the `.plist` format. Sweet!

2. And if the Root element of your data is a Dictionary type, you must then use:

```
CCDictionary * _myData = CCDictionary::createWithContentsOfFileThr
eadSafe(levelsFile.c_str());
```

3. Then when we need to load the dictionary for each level, now stored inside the _levels array, we do this:

```
CCDictionary * levelData = (CCDictionary *) _levels-
>objectAtIndex(_currentLevel);
```

> If we divide the levels into multiple `.plist` files, then we would need logic to refresh the _levels array each time a new `.plist` file is loaded.

And that's it for the loading and parsing. Now we can proceed to retrieving data for our level.

Each level dictionary starts with the data regarding the level's gravity (a level may start with a different gravity value), the start point where the player should be placed and the end point where the igloo should be placed.

4. These value are retrieved like this in our code:

```
_gravity = levelData->valueForKey("gravity")->intValue();
switch (_gravity) {
    case kDirectionUp:
        _world->SetGravity(b2Vec2(0,GRAVITY));
```

```
            break;
        case kDirectionDown:
            _world->SetGravity(b2Vec2(0,-GRAVITY));
            break;
        case kDirectionLeft:
            _world->SetGravity(b2Vec2(-GRAVITY, 0));
            break;
        case kDirectionRight:
            _world->SetGravity(b2Vec2(GRAVITY, 0));
            break;
    }

    _player->setSpritePosition(ccp(
        levelData->valueForKey("startx")->floatValue() * TILE,
        levelData->valueForKey("starty")->floatValue() * TILE
    ));

    _igloo->initIgloo(_gravity, ccp(
        levelData->valueForKey("endx")->floatValue() * TILE,
        levelData->valueForKey("endy")->floatValue() * TILE
    ));
```

5. Inside this same dictionary we have an array for platforms and an array for gravity
switches. These are retrieved like this:

```
CCArray * platforms = (CCArray *) levelData-
>objectForKey("platforms");
CCArray * switches = (CCArray *) levelData-
>objectForKey("switches");
```

6. These arrays contain yet more dictionaries containing data for the creation and
placement of platforms and gravity switches in each level. This data is passed to the
corresponding Platform and GSwitch classes and boom, you got yourself a level:

```
data = (CCDictionary *) platforms->objectAtIndex(i);
platform->initPlatform (
        data->valueForKey("width")->intValue() * TILE,
        data->valueForKey("angle")->floatValue(),
        ccp(data->valueForKey("x")->floatValue() * TILE,
        data->valueForKey("y")->floatValue() * TILE)
        );

data = (CCDictionary *) switches->objectAtIndex(i);
gswitch->initGSwitch(
        data->valueForKey("gravity")->intValue(),
        ccp(data->valueForKey("x")->floatValue() * TILE,
        data->valueForKey("y")->floatValue() * TILE)
        );
```

What just happened?

Parsing and retrieving data from a `Property List` file is a breeze with Cocos2d-x. You will always work with either an array of values or a dictionary of values and so the commands are very straightforward and familiar.

Saving game data

When planning your games you may soon decide you wish to store data related to your application, such as highest score or user preferences. In Cocos2d-x you can do this by simply accessing the `CCUserDefault` singleton.

With `CCUserDefault` you can store `integers`, `floats`, `doubles`, `strings`, and `boolean` with just one simple call per data type. For example:

```
CCUserDefault::sharedUserDefault()->setIntegerForKey(levelsComplete
d, _levelsCompleted);
CCUserDefault::sharedUserDefault()->flush();
```

The other methods are `setFloatForKey`, `setDoubleForKey`, `setStringForKey`, and `setBoolForKey`.

To retrieve data you use their respective getters.

I'll show you next how to use that in our game.

Time for action – storing the completed levels

Open the `LevelSelectLayer` class.

1. This is how the number of levels completed is retrieved, inside the layer's contructor:

   ```
   _levelsCompleted = CCUserDefault::sharedUserDefault()->getIntegerF
   orKey("levelsCompleted");
   ```

2. Initially `_levelsCompleted` will equal 0 if no data is present yet. So we store level 1 as "unlocked".

   ```
   if (_levelsCompleted == 0) {
       _levelsCompleted = 1;
       CCUserDefault::sharedUserDefault()->setIntegerForKey("levelsCo
   mpleted", 1);
       CCUserDefault::sharedUserDefault()->flush();
   }
   ```

3. Then whenever we start a new level, we update the number of levels completed, if the new level number is larger than the value stored:

```
if (_currentLevel > _levelsCompleted) {
    _levelsCompleted = _currentLevel;
    CCUserDefault::sharedUserDefault()->setIntegerForKey("levelsCo
mpleted", _levelsCompleted);
    CCUserDefault::sharedUserDefault()->flush();
}
```

> You don't have to `flush` the data each time you update it. You may group multiple updates under one `flush`, or find a spot in your logic where you can safely `flush` updates before exiting the app. CCNodes come with extremely helpful methods for this: `onEnter, onExit, onEnterTransitionDidFinish, onExitTransitionDidStart`.

What just happened?

For small bits of data related to your game, settings and preferences, `CCUserDefault` is an excellent way to store information. Cocos2d-x will once again map this to whatever local storage is available in each target system.

Using notifications in your game

This is one of my favorite Objective-C features ported to Cocos2d-x through the advent of the `CCObject`: notifications.

If you ever worked with an MVC framework or developed a game AI system you are probably familiar with a design pattern called the *Observer Pattern*. This consists of a central message dispatcher object other objects can subscribe to (observe) in order to listen to special messages; or in order it to dispatch their own messages to other subscribers. In other words: an event model.

With Cocos2d-x this is done very quickly and easily. Let me give you an example used in Eskimo.

Time for action – using CCNotificationCenter

If we want the `Platform` sprite to listen to the `NOTIFICATION_GRAVITY_SWITCH`, special notification all we need to do is add the `Platform` sprite as an observer.

1. Inside the `Platform` class, within the constructor you will find this line:

```
CCNotificationCenter::sharedNotificationCenter()-
>addObserver(this, callfuncO_selector(Platform::onGravityChanged),
NOTIFICATION_GRAVITY_SWITCH, NULL);
```

And yes, it is one line of code!

2. The message, or notification, `NOTIFICATION_GRAVITY_SWITCH` is created as a defined string in the `GameConfig.h` header file:

```
#define NOTIFICATION_GRAVITY_SWITCH "gravity switch"
```

The call to `CCNotificationCenter` tells it that the `Platform` objects will listen to this defined message, and when such message is dispatched every `Platform` object will call the `onGravityChanged` method.

3. In the game each gravity switch is color coded. When the eskimo hits a switch, the platforms texture changes to reflect the new gravity by switching to the color of the activated gravity switch. All done through a simple notification we dispatch inside `GameLayer` when collision with a `GSwitch` object is detected inside the main loop:

```
CCNotificationCenter::sharedNotificationCenter()-
>postNotification(NOTIFICATION_GRAVITY_SWITCH, (CCObject*)_
gravity);
```

We can also send some data along with the notification; in this example an `integer` value is briefly converted to a `pointer` value, indicating the new `_gravity` value.

4. When `Platforms` are destroyed we unsubscribe them inside their destructor:

```
CCNotificationCenter::sharedNotificationCenter()-
>removeObserver(this, NOTIFICATION_GRAVITY_SWITCH);
```

 Be aware this has nothing to do with push notifications. You use `CCNotificationCenter` to make your various game elements more aware of each other and to organize project wide responses to user input for instance, of special game conditions.

What just happened?

You have just learned how to make your life as a developer much, much easier. Adding an application-wide event model to your game is a powerful way to improve flow and interactivity between objects, and it's so simple to use that I'm sure you'll soon implement this feature in all your games.

Using the accelerometer

Now let's move to the few new topics related to gameplay. The first of which is the use of accelerometer data. Again, nothing could be simpler.

Time for action – reading accelerometer data

Just as you do with the `touch` events, you need to tell the framework you want to read accelerometer data:

1. You tell the framework you wish to use the accelerometer with a simple call inside any `CCLayer`:

```
setAccelerometerEnabled( true );
```

2. This causes the framework to call the following event handler which you must declare and implement:

```
virtual void didAccelerate(CCAcceleration* pAccelerationValue);
```

3. Accelerometer data is usually processed on a separate thread, so it's important to bring it to your main loop when you decide to use this data. In Eskimo, the accelerometer data changes the value of a `CCPoint` vector called `_acceleration`:

```
void GameLayer::didAccelerate(CCAcceleration* pAccelerationValue)
{
    _acceleration = ccp(
    pAccelerationValue->x * ACCELEROMETER_MULTIPLIER,
    pAccelerationValue->y * ACCELEROMETER_MULTIPLIER
    );
}
```

This value is then read inside the main loop and used to move the Eskimo. In the game only one axis is updated at a time, depending on the current gravity. So you can only ever move the Eskimo on the X axis or the Y axis with the accelerometer data, but never both at the same time.

Keep in mind there is also a Z axis value in the pAcceleration data. It might come in handy someday!

What just happened?

Yep. With a couple of lines you added accelerometer controls to your game.

It is common practice to add extra filters to these accelerometer values, as results may vary between devices. These filters are ratios you apply to pAccelerationValue to keep values within a certain range, and you can find a variety of formulas for these ratios online. This will depend on how sensitive or responsive you need the controls to be.

In the game, we only update the eskimo with the accelerometer data if the sprite is touching a platform. We can quickly ascertain that by checking the _player's body contact list, if it exists or not:

```
if (_player->getBody()->GetContactList())
```

Reusing b2Bodies

In Eskimo we have a pool of b2Bodies used inside the Platform objects and we also change the shape of the little eskimo whenever the player taps the screen. This is possible because Box2D makes it very easy to change the fixture data of a b2Body fixture, without having to destroy the actual body.

Let me show you how.

Time for action – changing a b2Body fixture

All you have to do is make a call to the ->DestroyFixture method of b2Body. Not surprisingly, this should be done outside the simulation step:

1. Inside the methods makeCircleShape and makeBoxShape in the Eskimo class you will find these lines:

```
if (_body->GetFixtureList() ) {
    _body->DestroyFixture(_body->GetFixtureList());
}
```

Here we just state, if there is a fixture for this body, destroy it. We can then switch from a box to a circle fixture when the player taps the screen, but use the same body throughout.

2. We use this feature with platforms also. Platforms inside the pool that are not being used in the current level are set to inactive:

```
_body->SetActive(false);
```

This removes them from the simulation.

3. And when they are reinitialized to be used in a level we destroy their existing fixture, update it to match the data from the `.plist` file, and set the body to active once again.

```
//Define shape
b2PolygonShape box;
box.SetAsBox(width * 0.5f /PTM_RATIO, PLATFORM_HEIGHT * 0.5f /
PTM_RATIO);

//Define fixture
b2FixtureDef fixtureDef;
fixtureDef.shape = &box;
fixtureDef.density = 1;
fixtureDef.restitution = 0;

//reutilize body from the pool: so destroy any existent fixture
if (_body->GetFixtureList()) {
    _body->DestroyFixture(_body->GetFixtureList());
}

_body->CreateFixture(&fixtureDef);
_body->SetTransform(b2Vec2(position.x / PTM_RATIO, position.y /
PTM_RATIO), CC_DEGREES_TO_RADIANS(-angle));
_body->SetActive(true);
```

What just happened?

So just as we've been doing with pools of CCSprites, we can apply the same logic to b2Bodies and never instantiate anything inside the main loop.

And that's all folks!

Play the game. Check out the source code (that is chock-full of comments). Add some new levels and make the little eskimo's life a living hell!

Have a go hero

The gameplay for Eskimo could be further improved with a few new ideas that would force the player to make more errors.

It is a common feature in these type of games to evaluate the degree of "completeness" in which a level was played. There could be a time limit for each level, and items for the eskimo to pick up. The player could be evaluated at the end of each level and awarded a bronze, silver, or golden star based on his or her performance. And new groups of levels may only be unlocked if a certain number of golden stars were acquired.

Summary

Yes, you have a cool idea for a game, great! But a lot of effort will go into structuring and optimizing it. Cocos2d-x can help with both sides of the job.

Yes, CCScenes can be a bit cumbersome depending on your needs, but they are undisputed memory managers. When CCDirector kills a scene, it kills it dead.

Loading external data can not only help with memory size, but also bring in more developers into your project, focusing specifically on level design, and the external data files that create them.

And notifications can quickly become a must in the way you structure your games. Pretty soon you will find yourself thinking in terms of notifications and events to handle game states and menu interactivity, among other things.

Now, all we need to talk about is portability.

10

Code Once. Retire.

Cocos2d-x projects can target a variety of systems, including all the major players in the smartphone world. But can we code only once and run our project everywhere? Yes and no. The worst-case scenario is: if you target six different devices, you might have to add logic specific to each device and package the project in six different ways. Although the code may remain the same throughout, and the core logic of your game will certainly remain the same, you may have to add conditionals inside your code, tackling issues relating to the different targets. Images may need to be packed differently as well; the same goes for sound files. Again, this is a worst-case scenario.

It is also possible that some features cannot be ported to every system, particularly those related to external APIs or services. But what this means is, that you are left with the other 99.9 percent of project ideas that you can implement successfully on multiple targets!

In this final chapter, you will learn:

◆ How to create an Android project with Cocos2d-x

◆ How to compile C++ code in Eclipse.

◆ How to create an iOS/Android hybrid project

◆ How to create a Box2D iOS/Android hybrid project

First, a word on versions and requirements

The tutorials detailed in this chapter are all based on the following software versions:

- Eclipse Indigo 3.7.2
- Cocos2d-2.0-x-2.0.4
- NDK r8d

Some of the menu names, button labels, and wording on options and messages might change if you have different versions of the software listed above (especially Eclipse); this does not mean that things won't work, it only means you may have to spend a few extra seconds translating the instructions to your system.

Also, all of the steps shown here were performed on a Mac. But, again, you should have no problem translating them to your machine.

Requirements

It is assumed that you have Eclipse installed (`www.eclipse.org`) and a current version of the Android SDK (`http://developer.android.com/sdk/index.html`) already set up within Eclipse.

You should download the current Native Development Kit from `http://developer.android.com/tools/sdk/ndk/index.html`, and please make a note of where you placed each of these elements in your system.

I like to place the Android SDK and NDK inside the **eclipse** folder in **Applications**, so I can move it all later if I wish to make a backup. So, in my system, I have something like:

It is also assumed that you know how to create an Android virtual device in Eclipse. In case you don't, there are number of videos on YouTube for this very topic. I just don't want to be too sidetracked in these tutorials, as they cover a lot of steps already.

Further steps

You might want to edit the paths inside your system to include the NDK directory with an alias of NDK_ROOT, and a path to the Cocos2d-x directory with an alias of COCOS2DX_ROOT. In a Mac, this would involve editing the .bash_profile file.

This is optional, however, as I'll cover the steps working on the assumption that you do not have these paths in your system. But in the future, this could save time.

So let's start by creating an Android project.

Time for action – creating an Android project with Cocos2d-x

1. Go to the Cocos2d-x framework directory. This is the same one that we've been using to check on the test projects, only now you want to open the create-android-project.sh file in a text editor of your choice. (Also notice the other scripts for the various targets.)

2. Look for where the paths for NDK_ROOT and ANDROID_SDK_ROOT are being set.

3. Change the values there to the paths in your system. Since I have mine inside the **eclipse** folder in **Applications**, it looks like this:

   ```
   # set environment parameters
   NDK_ROOT_LOCAL="/applications/eclipse/android-ndk-r8d/"
   ANDROID_SDK_ROOT_LOCAL="/applications/eclipse/android-sdk-macosx/"
   ```

4. Save the file and close it. Now open Terminal.

5. Type in cd (that is, cd and a space).

6. Drag the framework folder to the Terminal window; mine says cocos2d-2.0-x-2.0.4.

7. Hit *Enter*.

8. Now type in the following line:

   ```
   ./create-android-project.sh
   ```

9. Hit *Enter*. You will be asked to enter a package name for your project. You will see the following line:

   ```
   Input package path. For example: org.cocos2dx.example
   ```

10. Do so, and hit *Enter*.

11. You will then be asked for a target ID; this is the Android version ID you are targeting. The window will also print all available IDs in your system before asking for one. (I usually enter a value of 9 or above, here.) Enter the ID and hit *Enter*.

```
input target id:
```

12. You will be required to enter a project name.

```
input your project name:
```

13. Name it whatever you like and hit *Enter*, and you're done.

What just happened?

You just created an Android project using a Cocos2d-x template. This will create a folder with the name of your project inside the Cocos2d-x framework root. If you go to that folder, you will see what's shown in the following screenshot:

What you see is an Android version of the `HelloWorld` project that we've seen before, inside Xcode. Now, let's compile the C++ code for our new project.

Time for action – compiling the code

1. Inside your new project folder, open the `proj.android` folder and find the `build_native.sh` file. Open this file in a text editor.

2. At the top of the file, below the first line where you find your project name, add this line:

```
NDK_ROOT="/applications/eclipse/android-ndk-r8d"
```

3. The path to NDK_ROOT should match the one in your system. If you have set up the PATH environment variable in your system for that folder, you may skip this step.

4. Save the file, and then close it.

5. Now open a new Terminal window.

6. Type in cd (that is, cd and a space) and drag the proj.android folder to the terminal window.

7. Hit *Enter*.

8. Now type in the following line:

```
./build_native.sh
```

9. Hit *Enter* again.

Sit back and relax while all of the C++ files in your project are compiled.

What just happened?

With these last steps, you compiled all of the C++ code of your new project using the NDK. Right now, this includes only the code from the Cocos2d-x framework, as we haven't added any of our own classes.

But what if you want to use an IDE to compile the code instead? We'll do that next.

Using Eclipse

So now we need to prepare Eclipse for our C++ project, as we need to compile the necessary Java code to run our Android project.

If you recall, when creating a Cocos2d-x project in Xcode, we are left with some Objective-C code that is required as the necessary link between our C++ logic and iOS.

The same thing happens with the Android project, but in this case it's Java code.

Now let's set up Eclipse to handle our C++ code.

Time for action – installing the C++ compiler

1. In Eclipse, go to **Help | Install New Software**.

2. In the drop-down list for **Work with:**, select your Eclipse version. Mine is Indigo.

3. You will need to select items from the categories **Mobile and Device Development** and **Programming Languages**.

4. Look for the following items, or similarly named items:

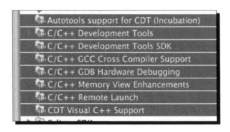

5. Proceed with the installation. You might need to restart Eclipse.

What just happened?

We just installed the extra software that is needed to compile C++ code in Eclipse. But we are not yet done with setting up the IDE.

Time for action – adding the Cocos2d-x library to Eclipse

1. In Eclipse, go to **File | Import**.

2. Choose **Existing Projects into Workspace**.

3. In **Select root directory**, click on **Browse** and navigate to the `cocos2dx/platform/android/java` folder inside the Cocos2d-x framework root.

4. Click on **Finish**.

5. This should load the Cocos2d-x library inside your workspace, under the name **libcocos2dx**.

What just happened?

This step will make working with Cocos2d-x in Eclipse a bit easier as we will now be able to link our projects to the Cocos2d-x library. It's time to bring our brand new Android project to Eclipse.

Time for action – opening the project in Eclipse

1. Go to **New | Project...**.

2. Under **Android**, select **Android Project from Existing code**.

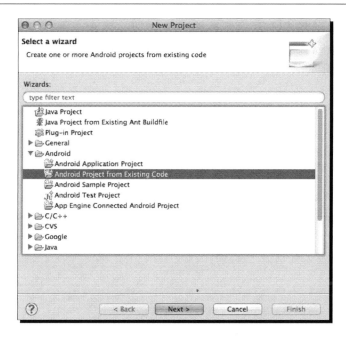

3. Click on **Next**.

4. For **Root Directory**, browse to the `proj.android` folder inside the project that you created a few steps back.

5. Click on **Finish**.

6. Link the project to the Cocos2d-x library. With your project selected, go to **Project | Properties**, then **Java Build Path**, then the **Projects** tab. Click on **Add...**, and select the previously-loaded libcocos2dx project. Click on **OK**.

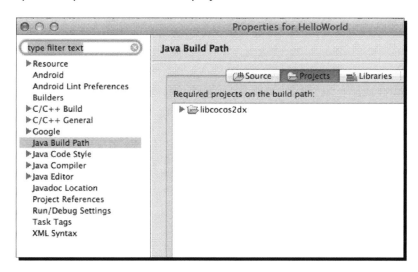

What just happened?

We opened our project in Eclipse. We always do so by importing the `proj.android` folder generated by the script that created the android project.

If Eclipse tells you that there are missing resource files listed in the manifest, it probably means that the icon file is named differently. In `AndroidManifest.xml`, change the word `icon` in `@drawable/icon` to whatever is stored in the `res` folders.

Running the application

With your project selected, choose **Run | Run As... | Android Application**.

You should see something like the following image in your emulator:

If you wish to use the emulator, build one with a 320 x 480 pixel screen, with the ARM processor and targeting Version 4.1 of the SDK (the test application looks better on an iPhone-size screen.) Then, make sure that you select the **Use Host GPU** option. Since our version of Cocos2d-x uses OpenGL ES 2.0, we need these settings to test our code in the emulator. However, this does not mean that the emulator will always work. *It is always best to test on a device.*

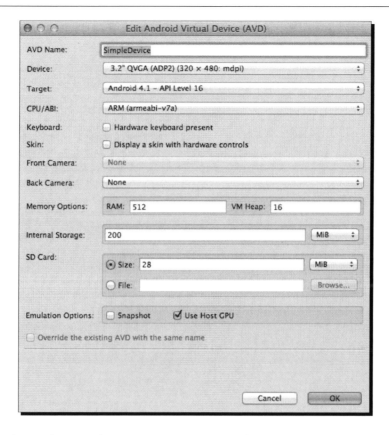

You also need to make sure that `minSdkVersion` inside `AndroidManifest.xml` reflects this requirement, so set the value to something above `9`, and preferably above `11`. Then open **Properties**, and under **Android**, select **Android 3.1** as the target. I don't know why, but this is the only way, I've found, to use the emulator with OpenGL 2.0. Again, testing on a device is the best thing to do when developing for Android, especially when using OpenGL 2.0.

Also, make sure that you click on **Add** in the **Library** section and select our libcocos2dx project, if it's not already listed there.

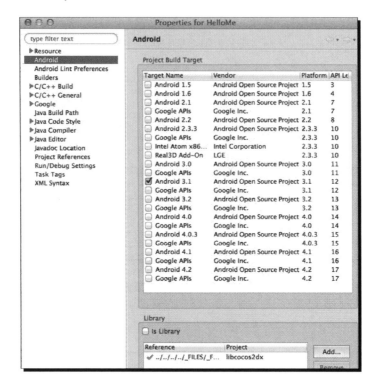

Now if you make changes to the C++ code—for instance, change the **Hello World** label—you would have to once again run `build_native.sh` inside Terminal, by repeating the steps we performed a few moments ago.

The script only compiles updated classes, so it will run much faster. Or, you can skip all that and have Eclipse run the build script from now on.

Compiling C++ code in Eclipse

Technically speaking, we only need to install the CDT plugins in Eclipse to handle this step. But you'll be glad we did this. So let's use Eclipse to compile our C++ code.

Time for action – compiling our C++ code

1. In Eclipse, select your project. Then select **File | New | Other...**, and under **C/C++**, select **Convert to a C/C++ Project (Adds C/C++ Nature)**.

2. Click on **Next**. In the next window, we have to select our compiling tool chain.

3. Make sure that your project is selected under **Candidate for conversion:** (you don't have to select the libcocos2dx project), select **Makefile project** under **Project type:**, and select **Other Toolchain** under **ToolChains:**.

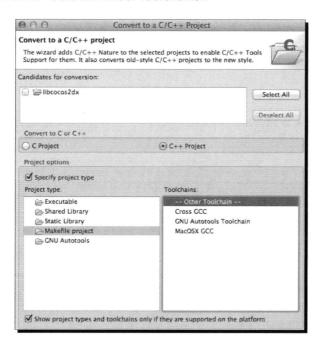

4. Click on **Finish**.

5. Once again, go to the **Properties** window for your project.

6. Under **C/C++ General**, select **Paths and Symbols**, and click on the **Includes** tab.

7. Select the option **GNU C++.**

8. Click on **Add**.

9. Click on the **File System...** button and look for the file system for your Cocos2d-x framework root, and choose `cocosd2dx/` and `/cocos2dx/include`.

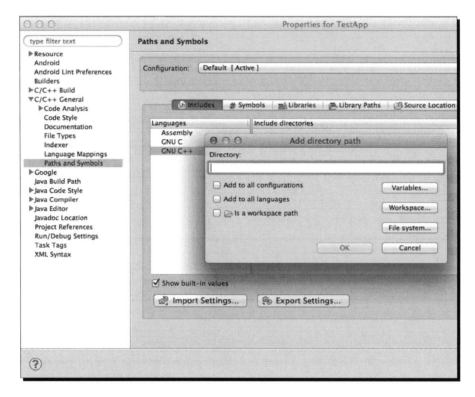

10. Add a third include and search inside your NDK root folder for `ndk/platforms/android-14/arch-arm/usr/include/` or any version equal to 9 or above (so searching for `ndk/platforms/android-9/arch-arm/usr/include/` would work too). By the end of these steps, you should have three lines of includes in **Include directories**.

11. Select the **Source Location** tab, which is also in **Paths and Symbols**.

12. Click on **Link Folder....**

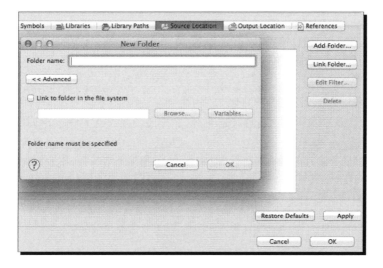

13. Select the option **Link to folder in the file system**, then click on **Browse** and browse to the **Classes** folder inside your project. This will show you the C++ classes of your project in Eclipse.

14. In the **Properties** dialogue box, go to the **C/C++ Build** option. Deselect **Use default build command**.

15. We can finally add our build script command line. In **Build command:**, type in the following line:

```
bash ${workspace_loc:/PROJECT_NAME}/build_native.sh
```

16. Make sure to replace **PROJECT_NAME** with the name of your project. Click on **Apply**.

17. We are not done yet! Go back to **C/C++ General** and select the **Code Analysis** option.

18. Select **Use project settings**. Inside the **Problems** box, deselect **Syntax and Semantic Errors**.

    This step may become optional in the future and Eclipse may learn to handle the syntax a little better. But for now, we need to block incorrectly identified errors.

19. Go to the **Classes** folder, select `HelloWorldScene.cpp`, and make some changes to the label or positioning. When you're done, go to **Project | Build All**, and watch as Eclipse compiles your new code. (You may need to clean the project before this, and restart Eclipse to be rid of errors.)

20. Run your application; you should see your changes in place.

What just happened?

We just told Eclipse how to handle our project. And yes, it took us twenty steps to do it! But fear not; we did cover a lot of ground.

We created our compiling tool chain, added paths to all the necessary libraries, brought a reference to our **Classes** folder to the IDE, told Eclipse to relax and not bother with too many warnings, and told it where to find our build script so we no longer need to use Terminal.

And now, step number twenty one is: go fix a cup of tea or something! You deserve it.

And many, many thanks to Jean-Yves Mengant for describing all of these steps in his wonderful online tutorial (`http://www.raywenderlich.com/11283/cocos2d-x-for-ios-and-android-getting-started`).

Creating a hybrid project

The steps for creating a hybrid project are very similar. We'll create an Android/iOS project here, but similar steps may be taken to add other targets.

Time for action – creating a hybrid Cocos2d-x project

1. Go to Xcode and create a Cocos2d-x project. Call it `HelloMe`.
2. Now go to the Cocos2d-x framework folder and repeat the steps to create an Android project; call it `HelloMe` as well. This will create a `HelloMe` folder inside the Cocos2d-x framework folder.
3. Go to that new folder and copy its `proj.android` directory.
4. Go to the `HelloMe` project folder you created in Xcode. This must be the system folder in Finder. Paste the `proj.android` directory inside the innermost `HelloMe` folder. After this, you can delete the `HelloMe` folder inside Cocos2d-x root.

5. Go to the Cocos2d-x framework folder again and copy the folders `cocos2dx`, `CocosDenshion`, and `extensions`.

6. Go to the Xcode `HelloMe` project folder in Finder, and copy and paste it in the `libs` folder. When asked if you wish to replace the current folder, click on **Yes**.

7. Go inside the `proj.android` folder and open the `build_native.sh` file (in a text editor).

8. Once again, add this line at the top: `NDK_ROOT="/applications/eclipse/android-ndk-r8d"`. This adds the actual path for your NDK.

9. This time, there is one more line that we need to edit here. Look for these lines:

   ```
   COCOS2DX_ROOT="$DIR/../libs"
   APP_ROOT="$DIR/.."
   APP_ANDROID_ROOT="$DIR"
   ```

   Make sure the first one reads as the one shown previously. What we are doing here is telling the build script to look for the framework source code inside the `libs` folder of our project.

10. From here on, you should follow the same steps as before. Run the build script, load this project into Eclipse, make all the necessary changes to the project as we've done before, and compile the code.

What just happened?

With these simple steps (plus all of the previous ones), you can create a hybrid Android/iOS project. Now you can open the same project inside Xcode (though you might need to clean it up first) or Eclipse. You can even work with both IDEs at the same time.

So now if you go to Xcode and change the label in `HelloWorldScene.cpp` to read **Hello Me**, Eclipse will warn you that the file was changed and update its own opened copy of the project.

Build the project in Eclipse and run it in the Android simulator. (Again, make sure you set the target correctly for the emulator.) You should be able to see the changes applied.

If you want to add more targets, you will need to create these inside the Cocos2d-x framework folder and drag `proj.TARGET_NAME` to this `HelloMe` project folder (just as we've done with `proj.android`), and then make all the necessary changes so that the Cocos2d-x source code can be found by the new targets.

Creating a Box2D hybrid project

The steps are, again, very similar. You only need to make sure that you add the Box2D library to your project. Let me show you how.

Time for action – creating a Box2D project

1. Create a Box2D project in Xcode. Call it `Box2dHello`.
2. Create an Android project with the same name; only this time, use the argument `-b` to build a Box2D project:

   ```
   ./create-android-project.sh -b
   ```

3. Drag the `proj.android` folder to the Xcode project folder in Finder, like we did in the previous set of steps.

4. Drag copies of the folders `cocos2dx`, `CocosDenshion`, `extensions`, and `Box2D` (you'll find these inside the `externals` folder in the the Cocos2d-x framework root) to the `libs` folder of your project.

5. Follow the remaining steps to set up the project in Eclipse. Then open the file `proj.android/jni/Android.mk`.

6. Edit `LOCAL_C_INCLUDES` to include the Box2D library:

   ```
   LOCAL_C_INCLUDES:= $(LOCAL_PATH)/../../libs/Box2D \
   $(LOCAL_PATH)/../../Classes
   ```

   Notice how the path points to the folders inside the `libs` folder.

7. You may have to edit the last line in the `Android.mk` file to read:

   ```
   $(call import-module,Box2D)
   ```

Now you are ready to run the project.

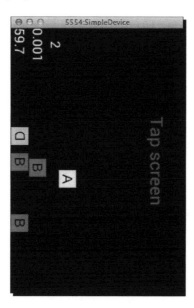

What just happened?

You created a hybrid Android/iOS project with Box2D support. And now for our last trick, a word or two on working on a hybrid project, and off you go!

Developing a hybrid game

When working with a hybrid project, make sure you constantly test all of its target versions, as there are things that each target may or may not allow. For instance, we used spaces in some of the project names that we created in Xcode; Android, however, will not allow that.

Besides this, the debugger inside Xcode will act differently at times compared to the NDK. The latter may require more `include` statements than the former. The NDK may signal more errors inside Eclipse than the debugger inside Xcode.

It's important to catch these distinctions early and not let them accumulate.

Other than the steps listed in this chapter, you will also need to keep updating the `Android.mk` file inside the `jni` folder in `proj.adroid` with every new class that you add, by changing the list in `LOCAL_SRC_FILES`.

For instance, the `LOCAL_SRC_FILES` entry in the `Android.mk` file for the game MiniPool would read:

```
LOCAL_SRC_FILES := hellocpp/main.cpp \
                   ../../Classes/AppDelegate.cpp \
                   ../../Classes/Block.cpp \
                   ../../Classes/GameSprite.cpp \
                   ../../Classes/Player.cpp \
                   ../../Classes/Terrain.cpp \
                   ../../Classes/GameLayer.cpp
```

Also, the last `#include` in `main.cpp`, which you find in `proj.android/jni/hellocpp/`, should point to `GameLayer` in that example:

```
#include "GameLayer.h"
```

Keep the Cocos2d-x macros in mind, to help you code target-specific logic within your game:

```
if (CC_TARGET_PLATFORM == CC_PLATFORM_IOS)
if (CC_TARGET_PLATFORM == CC_PLATFORM_ANDROID)
if (CC_TARGET_PLATFORM == CC_PLATFORM_BLACKBERRY)
if (CC_TARGET_PLATFORM == CC_PLATFORM_WIN32)
if (CC_TARGET_PLATFORM == CC_PLATFORM_MAC)
if (CC_TARGET_PLATFORM == CC_PLATFORM_LINUX)
```

Summary

It may be easy to forget that you really only coded your game once when you're busy compiling your game for two platforms and submitting it to two different stores.

The work and hassle of producing and marketing a game will certainly seem to be multiplied by two. There are many things that you could blame for that, but it's certainly not Cocos2d-x. You will always be amazed at the number of measures taken by the people who developed the framework to ensure the effectiveness of your code.

Sure, it does seem like a lot of steps when you're adding Android (or Windows, or Bada for that matter) as a target. But soon enough, you'll be doing these steps with your eyes closed.

So, rock on! Keep it simple and fun. We, the players about to get squished and zapped in your awesome future games, salute you.

Vector Calculations with Cocos2d-x

The appendix covers some of the math concepts used in *Chapter 5*, *On the Line – Rocket Through*, in a little more detail.

What are vectors?

First, let's do a quick refresh on vectors and the way in which you can use Cocos2d-x to deal with them.

So what is the difference between a vector and a point? At first they seem to be the same. Consider the following point and vector:

◆ Point (2, 3.5)

◆ Vector (2, 3.5)

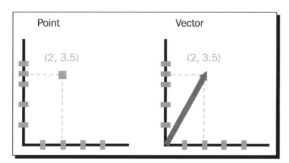

In the previous figure they each have the same value for x and y. So what's the difference?

With a vector you always have extra information. It is as if besides those two values for x and y, we also have the x and y of the vector's origin, which in the previous figure we can assume to be point (0, 0). So the vector is "moving" in the direction described from point (0, 0) to point (2, 3.5). The extra information we can derive then from vectors is direction and length (usually referred to as magnitude).

It's as if a vector is a person's stride. We know how long each step is, and we know the direction in which the person is walking.

In game development, vectors can be used, among other things, to describe movement (speed, direction, acceleration, friction, and so on) or the combining forces acting upon a body.

The vector methods

There is a lot you can do with vectors, and many ways to create them, and manipulate them. And Cocos2d-x comes bundled with helper methods that will take care of most of the calculations for you. Here are some examples:

- You have a vector, and you want to get it's angle: `ccpToAngle(vector)`
- You have an angle, and you want to transform it into a vector: `ccpForAngle(angle)`
- You want the length of a vector: `ccpLength(vector)`
- You want to subtract two vectors; for example, to reduce the amount of movement of a sprite by another vector: `ccpSub(vector1, vector2)`
- You want to add two vectors; for example, to increase the amount of movement of a sprite by another vector: `ccpAdd(vector1, vector2)`
- You want to multiply a vector; for example, applying a friction value to the amount of movement of a sprite: `ccpMult(vector1, value)`
- You want the vector that is perpendicular to another (also known as a vector's normal): `ccpPerp(vector)` or `ccpRPerp(vector)`
- And most importantly for our game example, if you want the dot product of two vectors: `ccpDot(vector1, vector2)`

Now let me show you how to use these methods in our game example.

Using ccp helper methods

In the example of *Rocket Through*, the game that we developed in *Chapter 5, On the Line – Rocket Through*, we used vectors to describe movement, and now I want to show you the logic behind some of the methods in Cocos2d-x that we used to handle vector operations, and what do they mean.

Rotating the rocket around a point

Let's start, as an example, with the rocket sprite moving with a vector of (5, 0).

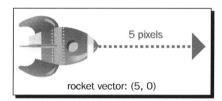

We then draw a line from the rocket, say from point **A**, to a point **B**.

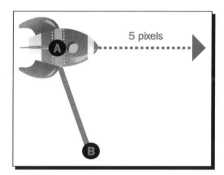

Now we want the rocket to rotate around point B. So how can we change the rocket's vector to accomplish that? With Cocos2d-x, we can use the helper point method `ccpRotateByAngle` to rotate a point around any other point. In this case we rotate the rocket's position point around point B by a certain angle.

But here's a question, in which direction should the rocket rotate?

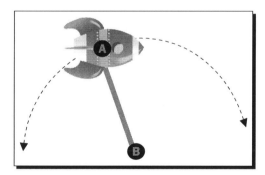

By looking at the previous figure, you know that the rocket should rotate clockwise, since it's moving towards the right. But programmatically how could we determine that and in the easiest way possible? We can determine this by using vectors and another property derived from them: the dot product.

Using the dot product of vectors

The dot product of two vectors describe their angular relationship. If their dot product is greater than zero, the two vectors form an angle smaller than 90 degrees. If it is less than zero, the angle is greater than 90 degrees, and if it is equal to zero, the vectors are perpendicular.

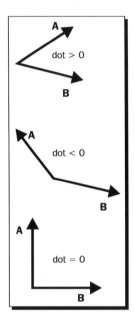

One other way to think about this is: if the dot product is a positive value, the vectors "point" to the same direction. If it is a negative value, they point to opposite directions. How can we use that to help us?

A vector will always have two perpendiculars, as shown in the following figure:

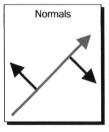

These perpendiculars are often called right and left, or clockwise and counterclockwise perpendiculars, and they are themselves vectors, known as normals.

Now if we calculate the dot product between the rocket's vector and each of the perpendiculars on line AB, you can see that we can determine the direction in which the rocket should rotate. If the dot product of the rocket and the vector's right perpendicular is a positive value, it means the rocket is moving towards the right (clockwise). If not, it means the rocket is moving towards the left (counterclockwise).

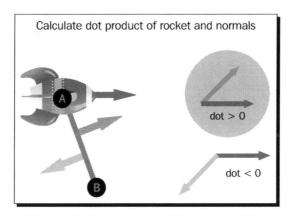

The dot product is very easy to calculate. We don't even need to bother with the formula, though it's a simple one, because we can use the `ccDot(vector1, vector2)` method.

So we have the vector for the rocket already. How do we get the vector for the normals? First we get the vector for the AB line. We use another method for this `ccpSub(point1, point2)`; this will subtract points A and B and return a vector representing that line.

Next, we can get the left and right perpendiculars of that line vector with the `ccpPerp(vector)` and `ccpRPerp(vector)` methods respectively. But we only need to check one of these. Then we get the dot product by using `ccpDot(rocketVector, lineNormal)`.

If this is the correct normal, meaning the value for the dot product is a positive one, we can rotate the rocket to point to this normal's direction; so the rocket will be at a 90 degree angle with the line at all times as it rotates. This is easy, because we can convert the normal vector to an angle by using the `ccpToAngle(vector)` method. All we need to do is apply that angle to the rocket.

But how fast should the rocket rotate? We'll see how to calculate that next.

Moving from pixel-based speed to angular-based speed

When rotating the rocket, we still want to show it moving at the same speed as it was when moving on a straight line, or as close to it as possible. How do we do that?

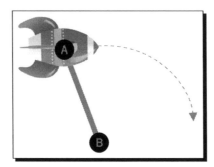

Remember that the vector is being used to update the rocket's position in every iteration. In the example I gave you, the (5,0) vector is currently adding 5 pixels to the x position of the rocket in every iteration.

Now let's consider an angular speed. If the angular speed were 15 degrees, and we kept rotating the rocket's position by that angle, it would mean the rocket would complete a full circle in 24 iterations, because 360 degrees of a full circle divided by 15 degrees equals 24.

But we don't have the correct angle yet, we only have the amount in pixels the rocket moves in every iteration. But math can tell us a lot here.

Math says that the length of a circle is *twice the value of Pi, multiplied by the radius of the circle*, usually written as *2πr*.

We know the radius of the circle that we want the rocket to describe: it is the length of the line we drew.

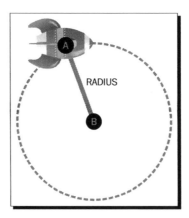

RADIUS

With that formula we can get the length in pixels of that circle, also known as its circumference. Let's say the line has a length of 100 pixels; this would mean the circle about to be described by the rocket has a length (or circumference) of 628.3 pixels (2 * π * 100).

With the speed described in the vector (5,0), we can determine how long it would take the rocket to complete that pixel length. We don't need this to be absolutely precise (the last iteration will most likely move beyond that total length) but it's good enough for our purposes.

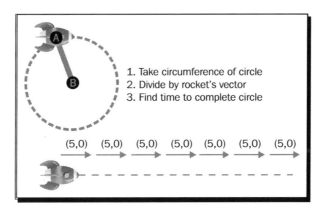

When we have the total number of iterations to complete the length, we can convert that to an angle. So if the iteration value is 125, the angle would be 360 degrees divided by 125, that is 2.88. This is the angle required to describe a circle in 125 iterations.

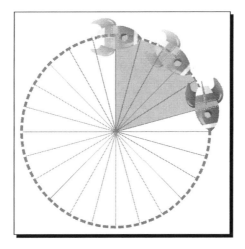

Now the rocket can change from a pixel-based movement to an angular-based movement without much visual change.

B
Pop Quiz Answers

Chapter 4, Fun with Sprites – Sky Defense

Pop quiz – sprites and actions

Q1	2
Q2	1
Q3	3
Q4	4

Chapter 8, Getting Physical – Box2D

Pop quiz – Box2D

Q1	3
Q2	2
Q3	1
Q4	3

Index

Thank you for buying
Cocos2d-x by Example Beginner's Guide

About Packt Publishing

Packt, pronounced 'packed', published its first book "*Mastering phpMyAdmin for Effective MySQL Management*" in April 2004 and subsequently continued to specialize in publishing highly focused books on specific technologies and solutions.

Our books and publications share the experiences of your fellow IT professionals in adapting and customizing today's systems, applications, and frameworks. Our solution based books give you the knowledge and power to customize the software and technologies you're using to get the job done. Packt books are more specific and less general than the IT books you have seen in the past. Our unique business model allows us to bring you more focused information, giving you more of what you need to know, and less of what you don't.

Packt is a modern, yet unique publishing company, which focuses on producing quality, cutting-edge books for communities of developers, administrators, and newbies alike. For more information, please visit our website: www.packtpub.com.

About Packt Open Source

In 2010, Packt launched two new brands, Packt Open Source and Packt Enterprise, in order to continue its focus on specialization. This book is part of the Packt Open Source brand, home to books published on software built around Open Source licences, and offering information to anybody from advanced developers to budding web designers. The Open Source brand also runs Packt's Open Source Royalty Scheme, by which Packt gives a royalty to each Open Source project about whose software a book is sold.

Writing for Packt

We welcome all inquiries from people who are interested in authoring. Book proposals should be sent to author@packtpub.com. If your book idea is still at an early stage and you would like to discuss it first before writing a formal book proposal, contact us; one of our commissioning editors will get in touch with you.

We're not just looking for published authors; if you have strong technical skills but no writing experience, our experienced editors can help you develop a writing career, or simply get some additional reward for your expertise.

[PACKT] open source *
community experience distilled

Cocos2d for iPhone 1
Game Development
Cookbook

Over 90 recipes for iOS 2D game development using cocos2d

Nathan Burba

Cocos2d for iPhone 1 Game Development Cookbook

ISBN: 978-1-84951-400-2   Paperback: 446 pages

Over 90 recipes for iOS 2D game development using cocos2d

1. Discover advanced Cocos2d, OpenGL ES, and iOS techniques spanning all areas of the game development process

2. Learn how to create top-down isometric games, side-scrolling platformers, and games with realistic lighting

3. Full of fun and engaging recipes with modular libraries that can be plugged into your project

Cocos2d for iPhone 0.99

Make mind-blowing 2D games for iPhone with this fast, flexible, and easy-to-use framework!

Beginner's Guide

Pablo Ruiz

Cocos2d for iPhone 0.99 Beginner's Guide

ISBN: 978-1-84951-316-6   Paperback: 368 pages

Make mind-blowing 2D games for iPhone with this fast, flexible, and easy-to-use framework!

1. A cool guide to learning cocos2d with iPhone to get you into the iPhone game industry quickly

2. Learn all the aspects of cocos2d while building three different games

3. Add a lot of trendy features such as particles and tilemaps to your games to captivate your players

4. Full of illustrations, diagrams, and tips for building iPhone games, with clear step-by-step instructions and practical examples

Please check **www.PacktPub.com** for information on our titles

Creating Games with cocos2d for iPhone 2

ISBN: 978-1-84951-900-7   Paperback: 388 pages

Master cocos2d through building nine complete games for the iPhone

1. Games are explained in detail, from the design decisions to the code itself

2. Learn to build a wide variety of game types, from a memory tile game to an endless runner

3. Use different design approaches to help you explore the cocos2d framework

Corona SDK Mobile Game Development: Beginner's Guide

ISBN: 978-1-84969-188-8   Paperback: 408 pages

Create monetized games for iOS and Android with minimum cost and code

1. Build once and deploy your games to both iOS and Android

2. Create commercially successful games by applying several monetization techniques and tools

3. Create three fun games and integrate them with social networks such as Twitter and Facebook

Please check **www.PacktPub.com** for information on our titles